For Des Sjoquist and Steve Beauchamp, dedicated colleagues and stormy weather friends, who understand that true democracy means openness to diversity of views in the search for creative solutions.

SAVAGE CAPITALISM AND THE MYTH OF

DEMOCRACY

Latin America in the Third Millennium

MICHAEL HOGAN

ISBN: 978-1-60145-953-4

Hogan, Michael, 1943—
Savage Capitalism and the Myth of Democracy

Library of Congress cataloguing information:

1.Globalization in Latin America. 2. Economic theory. 3. Latin America in the 21st Century. 4. Birth control. 5. Latin American History, 19th century. 6. Catholic Church in Latin America. 7. Twentieth century Latin American culture and politics. 8. The Green Revolution. 9. Coffee and micro-economics. 10. Fair Trade and Free Trade. 11. Urban gangs and gang intervention.

CREDITS

Some of these chapters first appeared in whole or in part as articles in various print and on-line magazines and sites. My thanks to the editors of *Monthly Review*, *Z Magazine* and *ZNet*, *Alterinfos*, *La Reforma* (Mexico City), *Sincronía* (Univ. of Guadalajara), The Washington Office on Latin America (WOLA), *Estudios Militares Mexicanos* (II Symposium Internacional de Historia Militar), Instituto Argentino para el Desarrollo Económico, Asamblea de Redes Cristianas (Madrid) and *Diario Casual* (Buenos Aires).

Table of Contents

INTRODUCTION

The genesis of this project was a conversation I had with Noam Chomsky in 2001 at the University of Guadalajara. I had been teaching in Mexico for more than a decade and Chomsky had just read my book *The Irish Soldiers of Mexico*. He commented that it contributed a great deal to the history of U.S. interventions in the region, which most citizens were only marginally aware of. We have since exchanged emails and commentaries on Central America, in which we share a common interest, and Colombia where both of us have visited often to speak to groups of students and educators.

My own students also encouraged this project, feeling—as so many young people do in Latin America—that the history of the region is little known to outsiders, and that European colonialism followed by 150 years of U.S. presence in the Americas has resulted in increasingly distorted perceptions.

I have worked as an educator in Latin America since 1990 when I was invited to come to Guadalajara, Mexico to teach. During the past six years in my post with the College Board in Latin America, I have visited Honduras, Barbados, El Salvador, Costa Rica, Nicaragua, Guatemala, Panama, Venezuela, Colombia, Chile, Paraguay, Uruguay,

Brazil and Argentina. In each country I spent several weeks (actually two months in Colombia) where I spoke with educators, university administrators and university students. In Central America I met also with gang leaders and law enforcement people. In addition, over the past twenty years I have visited most of the South and Central American republics several times, and written articles in both English and Spanish on a variety of subjects including politics, education, environmental issues and the arts of the region. While anyone who pretends to "understand" Latin America is a fool, I do attempt now and then to put my finger on the pulse of several trends or movements, and to provide them with historical perspective.

I am indebted to several remarkable historians and commentators who have gone before me. One cannot understand Mexico, for example, without absorbing Octavio Paz's *Labyrinth of Solitude*, or South America without reading Eduardo Galeano's *Open Veins of Latin America*. I freely acknowledge their influence and that of others throughout these chapters.

This book has no central organizing principle beyond recounting the continuous failures of colonial, imperialist and now neoliberal policies, and the hope which currently exists that several countries in Latin America have shaken off the chains and are slowly becoming self-actualizing in ways that the U.S. finds disturbing. What is presented to the reader is a series of occasional essays written during the past decade for alternative media, or as lectures for Latin American

2

students and teachers, in an effort to explore what has happened in the region (from the perspective of an academic and activist, an administrator and writer) as a result of neoliberal policies, an increasingly conservative Church, governments either wholly influenced by the U.S., the IMF and World Bank, or struggling (with the label "Marxist" or "populist") to provide security and a modicum of social services to their constituents. All of this in the wake of unprecedented gang violence, repressive police tactics, and levels of poverty and income disparity never before witnessed.

I have tried to be objective in my analysis. However, I should also note that objectivity for someone who lives here will seem very leftist to U.S. readers who are not yet weaned from CNN or Fox and who do not access alternative news media such as NACLA *Report on the Americas*, *Z Magazine*, *Monthly Review* and others. One cannot live in Latin America for any length of time, and still retain one's soul, without failing to be impressed by the damage caused by (1) the U.S. military interventions followed by abandonment (Nicaragua, El Salvador, Haiti); (2) the undermining of the democratic process (Guatemala, Chile); (3) the rapacious "free trade" policies (everywhere in the region); (4) active interference and external pressures in the electoral process (Mexico, Honduras, Nicaragua, Venezuela, Bolivia, Peru); (5) military buildups to intimidate the left, the students, and the reformists (Peru, Bolivia, Colombia, Paraguay), and (6) the failure of the Catholic Church (in a region where 95% are Catholic) to fulfill its social mission because of conservative pressures.

That said, this is also a book which I hope will appeal to an audience that is a bit broader than the traditional left wing: it should be of interest to students of the region, to Catholic Worker groups and liberation theologians, to professors and students of Latin American studies, and to the average reader who wants to know more about life in the Americas. I should also add that, despite the title, I am no ideologue or polemicist. When a workable policy was proposed such as that of President Bush on immigration, I applauded it. When a much-maligned program such as Plan Colombia had some positive results, I noted them. While I criticize the hierarchical Church, I do not neglect to point out that some dedicated clergy and lay people are doing good work throughout the region despite lack of support. In addition, while I recognize the dangers of populist leaders, I tend to adopt a wait-and-see stance, especially when those leaders appear to be mitigating the effects of unbridled capitalism and privatization of resources by relieving poverty, promoting education and, in short, leaving their countries better off than they found them.

Finally, I should note that in addition to the fine historians, journalists and fellow educators whom I quote in these essays, I am also indebted to members of the military in several countries, university administrators, public officials, college students, and representatives of the U.S. Department of State. All have helped me, some unwittingly, in crafting a clearer picture of Latin America in the new millennium.

Guadalajara, Mexico. 2009

CHAPTER I: FREE TRADE - A PRIMER

You can't get the truth from the press these days because television, newspapers and magazines are in the service of advertisers who, of course, are interested in preserving the status quo, and in maintaining a high level of consumption from those of us who attend to their pronouncements on which is the best car, the most stylish suit, the most successful economy, and the true political philosophy. What is particularly sad about all of this is that teachers and professors, who have been charged with telling our children the truth, especially about such things that might affect their system of values, are as uninformed as everyone else. So, when one reads in the *Wall Street Journal* that "democracy and free trade go hand in hand," few question the pronouncement. And few U.S. teachers or college professors would challenge that statement in any of their classes.

In fact, however, nothing could be further from the truth. Not only does free trade have nothing to do with democracy, but in most cases throughout history the two have been inimical. Free trade prospered only at the expense of democracy and the freedom of the majority. The United States in its first 150 years as a democratic republic was adamantly against free trade, while the imperialist nation of Great Britain was its most staunch proponent. Great Britain, after ensuring that its textile industry after years of protectionist legislation was the most powerful in the world, that it had the most developed ports and a high level of commercial specialization, promoted a worldwide system of free trade. Its intention was to use the rest of the developing world to supply it with raw materials while it exchanged these for manufactured goods. With a monopoly on insurance and freight, large financial institutions to broker credit, and control of the money market, Great Britain's chief export in the late 18th and early 19th centuries was "free trade." No one questions today that Great Britain was an imperialist nation, that its trade policies caused the Opium Wars, and that its intention was not freedom at all but domination of the world.

The United States, on the other hand, a new republic with fledgling industries in the 19th and early 20th centuries, had protective tariffs galore to protect the growth of its new companies. Consumers were not only urged to buy U.S. goods, but foreign products were subject to such high tariffs that imports were too expensive for most U.S. citizens to purchase, although the manufacturing costs were, in fact, much cheaper.

As the United States developed, using as its rationale for continental domination a doctrine of imperialist expansion known as "Manifest Destiny," the center of industrial power began to change. With the invasion and conquest of Northern Mexico (which included the ports of San Francisco and San Diego as well as the states of New Mexico, Arizona, California, Nebraska, parts of Kansas, Wyoming, Montana and Colorado), the United States controlled maritime access on both sides of the continent as well as rich agricultural and mineral lands in between. The agricultural frontier moved west and south and the industrial base was solidified in the North by the end of the Civil War. By the turn of the century its factories had multiplied their productive capacity eight times. The United States produced twice as much steel as Great Britain and ten times as many miles of railroad. By the end of World War II as bank credits became available and a wide market opened for U.S. goods in a ravaged Europe, the United States became a world power which now advocated the doctrine of free trade and free competition, at least for the rest of the world.

The International Monetary Fund emerged along with the World Bank, both U.S.-dominated institutions, to ensure that other countries would not impose restrictive tariffs, and also that no nation would take over essential industries but would keep them in the private sector, no matter how detrimental this might be to their own national security. (Mexico with its nationalized petroleum industry continues to be a thorn in the side of the U.S., but steps have been taken to ensure that more and more of this industry is controlled by interests favorable to the U.S.)

This policy has allowed the United States to exploit the natural resources of Latin American countries while at the same time making them debtor nations—despite their natural wealth in petroleum, copper, iron and rare metals. U.S. capital operates within these nations by appropriating essential sectors of the local industry; from there it ultimately dominates the rest. Anti-trust laws, which operate stringently in the United States, do not exist to prevent multinationals from doing in Latin America what would be actionable in the United States. Moreover, should a country try to pass such laws to protect local industry, the World Bank and the IMF operate to ensure that development credits or loans will suddenly be unavailable. Should a democratically-elected president wish to stop the plunder of his country (such as Allende did in Chile), he can be certain of retaliation by the United States whether through political assassination by proxy or through external manipulation of the market leading to economic crisis and the regime's ultimate demise. As a U.S. teacher working in Latin America, I labored for more than a decade in ignorance of these basic economic facts. How was it possible to take Paul A. Samuelson's classic course in economics, to go on to graduate school, and then to work abroad for a decade without this basic knowledge? Why this compulsion now to unravel the facts and present this new vision? It's much like looking at one of those drawings of a forest in which there is a girl concealed in the leaves of one of the trees. Unless you have a certain perspective and someone carefully points out the diverging lines from the general picture, you can look forever and not see the girl.

However, once the lines are pointed out to you, you cannot "un-see" her. She is there every time you look at the picture.

Thus, while I had a good understanding of economic principles, and a basic understanding of world trade, my picture had been dominated by the U.S. view, the prevailing perspective on the world economy. Since I was also tied into that view as a small investor in mutual funds, I had no incentive to look for any divergent lines. I was, in fact, an ardent supporter of the Northern American Free Trade Agreement (NAFTA) when it was first proposed. However, as the years passed and I saw that the results of NAFTA were higher levels of unemployment in Latin America, a widening of the gap between rich and poor, an increase in the concentration of wealth in the hands of a few, and the impoverishment and disenfranchisement of larger numbers of people, I began to see a divergent image develop on the photographic plate of free trade.

I did not know how to articulate this new awareness without seeming un-American, or being labeled socialist or Marxist. And yet as an educator who believes his highest calling is to teach the truth as he clearly sees it, I felt a moral obligation to begin to articulate as best I could the disparity between the dominant picture and the image that now, clearly, I could not un-see.

The first step and the most important was the concept with which I began this chapter. It is a mistake to connect economic systems with political systems in teaching or in communicating. One can be a

Nazi, a monarchist or a republican and believe in free trade. One can also be a Nazi, a monarchist or a republican and believe in protectionism. There is no connection between democracy and free trade whatsoever. It is not connected in any way with free elections, freedom of the press, or even free enterprise in any essential way. In fact, many people in many countries have freely voted against it, written against it, and good Republican businessmen and farmers have railed against it. Good Democratic labor groups have worked against it as well, as have environmentalists and human rights advocates.

Second, free trade is a misnomer. Essentially there is nothing free about it. It merely means that the dominant economic power in the relationship requires the poorer trading partner to sell its raw product at the cheapest possible price to him, so that he can refine and package it and sell it back to the poorer partner and to the rest of the world at the highest profit to himself. And he will use all the political, economic and (if necessary) military force to see that the weaker nation continues to do so. Failure to comply will be considered a threat to the dominant nation's "national security." It is what has been called at varies times and places "*laissez-faire*" capitalism, "unbridled" capitalism, and even "wild" and "savage" capitalism, the last of the above now in current usage in Latin America.

There are some parallels with the historical social conditions which *laissez-faire* capitalism provoked (detailed in the novels of Dickens and Steinbeck), and what is happening in Latin America today:

child labor, homeless people in the cities, overflowing prisons, pollution, concentration of wealth in the hands of the few, abuse of power, and labor as a commodity with Latin Americans replacing the Irish and Okies at the bottom of the economic ladder. The difference between *laissez-faire* capitalism in the late 19th and early 20th century in England and the United States and that of today is that the former was concentrated in individual countries with autonomous governments which had the power to impose by executive fiat necessary socialist and labor reforms which turned capitalist economies into mixed economies. Governments such as Teddy Roosevelt's broke up trusts and monopolies, limited the expansion of single entities and their domination of related industries, and set aside lands which could not be developed for industrial purposes. Franklin Roosevelt put caps on speculation, guaranteed bank reserves and currency, nationalized essential industries, established social security and guaranteed retirement. These "socialist" moves are what saved the United States and made it a livable country.

The "savage capitalism" of the 21st century, however, is global. Individual governments such as those in Bolivia, Mexico, Colombia, or Nicaragua, if they were to attempt to pass laws within their own countries similar to those pushed through by FDR in the 1930s, would find themselves painted with the brush of Marxism, deprived of vital credits or loans, or even (as is the case with Cuba) cut off from trade by means of an economic blockade. Thus, Mexico allows millions more to starve each year rather than default on payments of external loans. Half of its GNP goes to servicing these loans; to the detriment of social services, price supports for food staples, and national health and safety. As a result, more than half of the people in this nation (so rich in resources, talent, energy and will) consume less than the daily U.N. nutritional minimum. The problem is not that there are too many people in Mexico or too few jobs. The problem is that its wealth is being drained by an exorbitant and militant capitalism which exports Mexican raw material and then sells it back to the country. Multinationals "invest" in Mexico only when they get concessions they would not ask for and could not obtain in the United States, so that even Mexican "exports" consist in large part of multinationals simply returning to the dominant investor the goods they have made with Mexican raw materials and labor. Many of these products (including Ford automobiles) are then re-sold on the Mexican market at prices 20 to 40% higher than in the United States. In taking out more dollars than they bring in, these multinationals fuel the area's dollar hunger. This leads in turn to currency devaluations, making materials within the country even cheaper, lowering wages, bankrupting small producers, and creating an economic crisis. The economic crisis is then followed by bailout loans and credits from the U.S. or from the World Bank, which are only granted by the IMF if controls are in place to ensure that funds are diverted from tax relief or social services. Thus, the next generation is obliged to pay off these loans by "belt-tightening measures" such as denying their children education, nutritional food, and safe places to live. This is how free trade creates poverty in Latin America despite its ironic promise that it is engaged in the enterprise of "development".

There is a scene in Steinbeck's *Grapes of Wrath* in which an Okie farmer is being driven off the land. He points a shotgun at the agent who has ordered him off, and threatens to shoot him. The agent explains that it's not his fault; it's that of the Land and Cattle Company. When the farmer asks who's in charge of the Land and Cattle Company, the agent tells him that there's no point in shooting that man either. He simply takes his orders from the bank. When asked where the head of the bank is so he can shoot him, the agent says the bank president takes orders from the Board of Directors. Finally, the farmer yells in frustration, "Well, then who the hell *do* I shoot?" One can understand his frustration. There are young people in Latin America today growing increasingly frustrated as they see their parents' dreams fade, and fulfillment of their own even less likely. The answer is not in controlling immigration, the answer is not birth control, the answer is not in sending helicopters and riot control equipment to governments concerned with the civil disorder economic despair can bring. The answer is realizing that although the world economy is complex, the subject has been clouded by obfuscation and corporate rhetoric. It is time to break it down, simplify and clarify, so that we can begin to see ways to remedy it before it's too late. The Okie farmer did not kill the bank manager or anyone else, because the United States under Franklin Roosevelt developed a domestic social policy which resulted in a sustainable national economy and secure country for most of the 20th century. Similarly, in the 21st century we must search for ways we can come together to establish a sustainable global economy and a secure planet.

CHAPTER II: RX FOR HISTORICAL ENTROPY

Beginning with the Mexican War of 1846-1848, the United States actively pursued a policy of economic and military expansion throughout much of the 19th and early 20th century. This is a part of U.S. history that is little discussed and seldom referred to in the United States. Few U.S. high school or college students can name a single battle of the Mexican War, despite the fact that Mexico lost two-fifths of its territory and the U.S. grew by one third in that war. The conquest of the Mexican territories (which would ultimately result in the formation of the states of California, New Mexico, Colorado, lower Texas and Arizona, parts of Kansas and Wyoming) has not been forgotten by our neighbors to the south. Most Mexicans agree with Ulysses S. Grant, that "it was the most unjust war ever waged by a stronger nation against a weaker one." As an integral part of Mexican education, this history affects how North Americans are perceived. Any North American dealing with a Mexican on an issue of mutual security, who does not understand that the Mexican's history is both more informed and more personal on this matter, will certainly be at a disadvantage.

The emigration which continues from Mexico into the United States is, at least in part, a legacy of this war. Most of the Mexicans are crossing an artificially imposed "border" into former Mexican territories. The fact that this emigration is exacerbated by economic discrepancies between the two nations is not lost on Mexican leaders who understand that the economic inequality, too, is a legacy of the past. They also understand that immigration whether legal or illegal is a pressure valve for their own nation. The United States cannot afford to have a Mexico destabilized by revolution, or by the chaos which would result from millions of poor (*gente sin recursos*) held captive in the south by too strict a control of its northern borders.

The impunity with which the United States entered Mexico in the early 20th century, whether General John "Black Jack" Pershing's army on the trail of Pancho Villa, or the U.S. Navy in Veracruz in self-righteous indignation over the arrest of a drunken sailor, has not been forgotten. A perceived arrogance in pursuit of U.S. national interests at the expense of the autonomy of others is something our leaders, businessmen and cultural ambassadors need to be keenly aware of. However, such education has been sorely lacking. As a result, attempts to influence Mexican elections, correct discrepancies in its banking system, change the structure of its police force, and emasculate leaders by threatening to deny "certification" on drug enforcement issues, has hampered independent growth in that country and made generation after generation of intelligent, cultured and sympathetic Mexicans skeptical of even the best-intentioned U.S. policies.

Dangers to Hemispheric Security

The danger to both U.S. and Mexican security is not that these incursions occurred. It is that, while U.S. interventions are part of the history and the culture of these two nations, those interventions are virtually unknown in the United States except to a handful of graduate students in Latin American studies and specialists in international relations. The interventions mentioned above are reported in none of the high school history texts, and are barely a footnote in most college texts. As a result, most U.S. citizens in Mexico, conducting business, working for the DEA, employed by the embassies, teaching in American Schools, are "history deficient," with little hope of understanding a culture whose history has been systematically excised from their texts. Moreover, since that history does not exist for them, significant parts of Mexican culture remain enigmas. By doing away with the history and our nation's part in it, we have impoverished Mexico and become the most powerful agents of historical entropy in Mexico and Central America.

As an educator in Latin America who has worked in Mexico, Central America and Colombia for the past twenty years, I see the results of our failure to educate our citizens in the history of these regions. I see the contempt for the cultures, the assumed superiority, arrogance, and glibness of my fellow citizens in this area of the world. It does untold damage to our relations with these countries and seriously undermines (as we have seen most recently in Guatemala) the conditions requisite for peaceful social dynamics and for protection of human rights. Samuel Huntington in a recent issue of *Foreign Affairs* warned that in the eyes of most of the world, the United States is becoming a "rogue superpower"…and is considered "perhaps the greatest single threat to their societies." Commenting on this view Noam Chomsky in a recent *Harper's* article noted that "Americans who prefer a different image of their society might call for reconsideration…. The U.S. defiance of world order has become so brazen as to be of concern to even hawkish policy analysts."

The first step is the education of our populace in a true United States history which does more than simply laud the early years of the Republic and depict our national story as a glorious progression in the areas of human rights, freedom, tolerance of diversity, and respect for other nations.

The second step is an increased focus on the teaching of Latin American history in courses offered to students, especially—but not limited to—those preparing to go into the diplomatic service, those majoring in international business, international relations, and international law. By Latin American history, however, I mean original accounts or accurate translations of **their** histories, not bleached-out or self-justifying versions written by North American writers. Neither businessmen nor diplomats will make much progress if their education in this area is limited to a parochial view. International education should be just that, international—providing students with an in-depth look at the geography, culture, language and history of the nations with which they intend to do business.

Post NAFTA Changes and the Drug Wars

After one year of NAFTA, Mexico had a $12 billion trade deficit. Mexico's poorest group, unable to afford the basic *canasta* of milk and tortillas for marginal survival, had grown from 14 million to 21 million between 1990 and 1994. In that latter year, the peso fell from 3.40 to the dollar to 6.50. The Mexican meltdown had begun.

The U.S. and the International Monetary Fund came to the rescue, but the $52 billion bailout ($20 billion from the U.S.) would carry a price. In effect, ordinary Mexican citizens who did not contract the debt were condemned to suffer the austerity measures imposed by foreign creditors on the local economy. These measures included drastic cutbacks in public spending and social services, so that a large percentage of the GNP could be set aside to meet foreign debt reservicing and repayment. The price of tortillas (the basic comestible) rose 100% in the first 24 months of the crisis. According to a study by Banamex, 62 million Mexicans had a caloric intake below U.N. minimum nutritional standards. Social programs were eviscerated; $26 billion left Mexico in capital flight as the rich cashed in their chips and the poor were left to die in the streets, or take to the mountains and jungles—like the Zapatista Liberation Army—and prepare for the coming revolution. Comandante Marcos of the EZLN in Chiapas was sending out missives via the Internet that even the beleaguered Mexican middle class was reading. "This loan has been signed off in…blood," he noted, while President Clinton confirmed much the same thing as he complimented President Zedillo on his courage in imposing "hard measures" on the Mexican people in order to quickly pay off the U.S. portion of the loan.

"Free trade, NAFTA, foreign loans, economic development" by First World nations have "resulted in increased job insecurity, a rising crime rate, and growing social inequality in Latin America," according to James Fogarty, author of the *Liberation and Development: A Latin American Perspective*. Not without reason some Latin American critics are calling it *capitalismo salvaje*, which they fear will result in economic genocide, that is, the elimination of those who are superfluous to the economic model. Fogarty's suggestion is that we abandon the neoliberal, world capitalist and developmental models which have ravaged Latin America for a "more humanistic approach aimed at attacking the root causes of injustice, poverty and social unrest." He points out the success of alternative models such as that of Costa Rica which reduced its poverty level by two-thirds in the 1980s, a period during which poverty in the rest of Central America grew exponentially.

The Next Annexation

There are an estimated 20 million Mexicans and Mexican-Americans living in the U.S. There are another 3.7 million who are Hispanic in origin, émigrés from Guatemala, El Salvador, Nicaragua, Cuba, Costa Rica and Honduras. By the year 2020 it is estimated that they will constitute 50% of California's electorate, and Caucasians will be a minority. Ironically, the invasion by the United States and subsequent annexation of two-fifths of Mexico in the 1840s has been answered by a counter-invasion of the United States by Mexican immigrants in the 20th century. They and their Central American fellow-Hispanics bring with them a culture of resistance and struggle, a militancy which has spread from the United Farm Workers to the AFL-CIO, from strikes in Pennsylvania and New York, to school walk-outs of Proposition 187 in California. A group of people who were driven out of their own countries by (often U.S. supported) *mal gobierno*, they have developed a culture of resistance which has been transplanted in U.S. soil. This culture is quite "American" at its base; it is grass roots democracy in action. It is peaceful resistance, which our Constitution guarantees to protect.

Human Rights

Yet this same social action south of our borders is labeled "political unrest" and its democratic leaders are termed "leftists" and "Marxists" and dangers to our national security. The U.S. (with the exception of Kent State) has not in modern times used its military to suppress popular dissent within its own boundaries. However, it has no problem equipping governments for such activities south of its borders, and then turning a blind eye. Military officers throughout South and Central America have been trained by the International Education Program (MET) and at the School of the Americas in Fort Benning, Georgia. Senior officers have often studied at the U.S. Army's Public Relations School in Indianapolis. These men have become consumers of U.S. military technology and hardware in their own countries. And the U.S. arms industry, which sells $12 billion worth of weaponry a year worldwide, wants to expand this market.

But what does Mexico do with Blackhawk helicopters, rockets, grenades, Hueys, troop transport planes, Hummers, machine guns? It has no external enemies. Only two scenarios come to mind. The first is to help the U.S. fight its ongoing "war on drugs;" the second is to suppress dissent within its own borders. This latter scenario is even more compelling when one sees that the export list of military gear from the U.S. to Mexico includes water cannons, riot control gear, and electronic shock units. While pretending to encourage the "democratic process" which includes, according to Thomas Jefferson, "the right to alter or abolish" a government when it becomes destructive of the rights of the people, the U.S. has in fact clandestinely promoted violations of human rights in Latin America to preserve a semblance of order in those nations, and to prime the pump of free market arms sales.

Drug Wars

The war on drugs, which most of the world sees as a U.S. domestic problem, has been exported to Mexico and Central America, with often disastrous results for the human rights of the local populace, the sustainability of freedom, and the other nation's own security. With the FBI, DEA, INS, CIA, Customs Service, National Security Agency, and the DOD's National Imaging and Mapping Agency all operating on Mexican territory, the compromises of human rights, the violations of national sovereignty, and the temptations to use Mexico as a stooge for the Colombia cartels, are obvious. In 1994, for example, the DEA smuggled 5.4 tons of cocaine in and out of Mexico as part of a sting operation of the Cali cartel, without ever notifying the Mexican authorities.

No one in Mexico believes that the use of drugs in the United States is a Mexican problem. The will of the above-mentioned agencies to make it a Mexican problem provides a fount of abuses, with no legal limitations on the personnel involved, except for agency reprimands of officials involved for "excess of enthusiasm."

Change of Focus

We need to focus on examining the impact of the history of the United States and those of her neighbors to the south, studying the errors we have made by proceeding with policies which have not taken these divergent histories into account, and suggesting solutions based upon insights this study provides. In those cases (there are many) where no clear solutions are available, we need to prioritize policies which contribute to the long-term sustainability of those countries and thus to hemispheric security, rather than short-term economic advantage.

The *Maquiladora* Industry

One such threat to our security is the *maquiladora* industry. Over 2, 500 foreign-owned assembly plants now employ over a million Mexicans and account for half of Mexico's manufacturing exports and 38% of total exports. But these plants have taken so many young Mexicans from the interior of Mexico that there is no infrastructure to accommodate them. Raw sewage pours into Rio Grande affecting Texas; crime flourishes (statistics on the rapes and murders of young working girls in this area are the highest in all of Mexico); toxic chemicals leak into the aquifer which touches Arizona, and the California border is an environmental disaster zone. The maquiladora economy is also an immigration emergency in the making. What would happen if there was any disruption in this industry?

I realize that there is no "right" answer to any of the questions but the process of thinking these questions through and re-examining the histories from both sides, will be illuminating—and perhaps enlightening. One result will be to reawaken U.S. interest in the importance of Mexico and Central America, to replace indifference with understanding, prejudice with knowledge, and ultimately aid in the security of our hemisphere and the sustainability of those nations to the south we call our neighbors. As an U.S. teacher working abroad, it has been particularly distressing to me that the education we have in the history of other countries is not only minimalist but often biased. This is particularly tragic in Latin America where U.S. presence will continue to be significant in the 21st century. International education in the U.S. needs to provide students with a cross-cultural view of the impact of U.S. interventions and continued U.S. presence in Mexico and Central America, and to show how our past policies continue to affect the lives of U.S. citizens and their neighbors to the south.

Central American Immigration

While I have concentrated mostly on the Mexican problem in this brief overview, it is important to note that the displacement of large groups of Guatemalans, Nicaraguans and Salvadorans during the disturbances of the past thirty years has resulted in vast increases of refugees and in illegal emigration of those peoples to the United States. Since many of the illegals "pretend" to be Mexican in an effort to avoid deportation to their respective countries, those who are caught by U.S. authorities tend to be returned to Tijuana or Nuevo Laredo where they add to border problems and put increased pressure on the already debilitated infrastructure of those communities. Most, as soon as the opportunity presents itself, attempt to emigrate once again to the U.S.

The large numbers of Guatemalans, Salvadorans and Nicaraguans have radically changed the barrios of East L.A. and the Mission District in San Francisco to cite two well-known examples. In the sixties and early seventies these neighborhoods were mostly Mexican, highly socialized, with strong family values. They hosted block parties, Cinco de Mayo celebrations, fiestas and concerts which were attended by people of every race. Now these areas have developed into dangerous enclaves run by rival gangs of teenage hoodlums, most of whom are recent arrivals from Central America where family units have been destroyed by war, where schools have long been closed, and culture abandoned for mere survival of the fittest. The streets of L.A. and the San Francisco Mission District have inherited the whirlwind previous Central American policies have sown.

Tentative Solutions

My long-term goal as an U.S. educator working abroad, as a writer, and as a parent is to help create a deeper understanding of Mexico and Central America in order to make our own country safe and those countries self-sustaining; to deepen our awareness, and to motivate educators to act now to insure that future generations will inhabit a peaceful, healthy and culturally rich hemisphere which honors human life and human diversity. With that in mind I'd like to offer a few tentative solutions to historical entropy.

1. The United States should continue to encourage study abroad and intercultural exchanges with Latin American students.

2. The study of a second language should be a requirement in secondary schools in the U.S., and native speakers should be employed to provide intensive courses.

3. The United States should make Latin American history a required subject for students in universities studying international business, international relations, international management, and international education.

4. Study abroad programs sponsored by the State Department, private agencies and universities should add a history component to their offerings so that students will develop an understanding and respect for the host country and its culture.

5. American Schools abroad should require all teachers to attend intensive language courses before the end of their first year, and to take a course in the history of their sponsoring country by the second year of their contract.

6. Since North American teachers in Latin America serve the upper and middle classes in their schools, teachers should also be required to make a service commitment to the community in which they live so that they become aware of and participate in local education, helping those children who are less fortunate, and whose families do not have the resources to allow them to attend such schools.

7. U.S. businesses abroad should develop a social awareness policy which includes quarterly reports on the impact of their investment and development activities in the host countries, and their efforts to alleviate dislocations, poverty, environmental destruction, and unfair competition.

8. Consumers and investors in the United States need to be more attentive to the cost of their investments as well as the profits. None of us would accept dividends from a company which invested our money in sales of cocaine or money laundering schemes, no matter how high the returns. Yet, we unquestionably receive high returns from companies which destroy the rain forest, decimate indigenous people, eviscerate local industries, and impoverish entire nations. We must insist on frank disclosures.

9. To facilitate this process, the United Nations should create Investment Disclosure Criteria which rank multi-national corporations on a scale of one to ten, reflecting their positive or negative impact on local industries, the environment, human rights, child labor, contribution to local standards of living, and social responsibility. Such rankings would be part of the Disclosure to Investors which accompanies the stock offering, and would allow investors to make informed and responsible decisions.

10. Alternative models to the neoliberal free trade prototype should be explored and supported in Latin America. What this means, in effect, is that popular democratic leaders who seek to implement

social change in Latin American countries should not be stymied or undermined by rigorous developmental restrictions, nor active interference by more developed countries in their internal affairs.

The success of the United States economically and militarily has created a sense of superiority and arrogance which emboldens its leaders and many of its citizens to denigrate or demonize alternative cultures, systems and ideas. Because of this, the cognitive dissonance which arises in the best students of American schools abroad is significant and cannot be obviated either by clever cynics who see their mission as one of asserting U.S. hegemony, or the well-intentioned and Candide-like teachers who see U.S. values as the best in the world. In the case of the former, contempt for alternative cultures and histories undermine the teacher's effectiveness. With the latter, the students perceive a gap between the ideals of the U.S. and its actions, which convinces them that the teacher is either ignorant or gullible, or both.

The American school teacher abroad has the obligation to be candid and forthright, **and** to have a depth of understanding of the past, and a commitment to the present. This does not mean replacing idealism with cynicism. But it does mean tempering our previous judgments with a healthy skepticism, holding on to those values which are truly universal, and when called upon to affirm a tenet of economic, social or political agenda which is repugnant, dismissing what insults our intelligence or sense of justice.

CHAPTER III: COFFEE AND MICRO-ECONOMICS

What most U.S. citizens read about Colombia in their newspapers are stories of cocaine cartels and political assassination. When I left Mexico a few years ago to attend an educator's conference in Bogotá, I was given a State Department advisory warning me that security at the Bogotá airport was among the worst in the world. I was also informed that Colombia was one of the most dangerous countries in the Americas, and that terrorists operated with impunity even in the streets of the capital.

What I discovered when I arrived was something quite different. The airport was far more secure than those in Dallas or Chicago. Passengers once they passed the security checkpoint were not allowed back, regardless of the excuse. All luggage was x-rayed; carry-on luggage was subjected to a very rigorous hand-search by security personnel. There were armed soldiers at all checkpoints, and there were police with drug-sniffing dogs.

The city of Bogotá itself was safer than many U.S. cities (L.A. and Detroit to name two), although there was evidence of drug violence in the bombed out Justice Building where, in an attempt to assassinate a federal judge, the cartel had taken out the entire block a couple of years earlier. However, this made it no less safe than, say, Oklahoma City, where a similar explosion took place. I wonder how the U.S. would respond, if Great Britain or Germany ranked Oklahoma City as one of the most dangerous in the world because of terrorism, or, since 9/11, New York City?

History of Colombia-U.S. Relations

While visiting Bogotá I discussed the history of Colombia with a well-known Catholic university historian who, in the process of explaining the strained U.S.-Colombia relations at that time, reminded me that roots of animosity with the U.S. occurred a hundred years ago. Like most U.S. citizens I was taught little of the history of Latin America in high school or even college classes. I knew nothing from my U.S. history texts which would suggest any reason why Colombia might have historical reasons for resenting or even distrusting the U.S. But back in the days of Teddy Roosevelt (which is not so long ago in Colombian history as it is in ours because their history is much older), Panama was part of Colombia. When the Colombian Congress refused to ratify the Hay-Herrán treaty to give the United States a 99 year lease across the Isthmus of Panama, President Roosevelt, and certain Panamanians who sought to make a profit, became indignant. A revolt in Panama, encouraged by the U.S., quickly broke out. Roosevelt, who just happened to have ordered the Great White Fleet off the coast of Colombia, used the Navy to prevent national troops from quelling the revolt. Three days later a revolutionary junta declared the independence of Panama from Colombia, and the Republic of Panama was officially recognized by the United States, thus freeing investors to begin the construction of the Panama Canal.

Respect for the autonomy of independent states in Latin America has never been one of the strong points of U.S. diplomatic policy. The latest U.S. effort, according to the professor, involved U.S. diplomatic maneuvers to change the Colombian Constitution to allow extradition of Colombian nationals to the United States to face U.S. justice for money laundering and/or conspiracy to transport drugs. The right of another country to punish one's own citizens is something few countries would acknowledge. Colombians are outraged that their government is even considering it, but in fact it seems to be a *fait acompli*. In an effort to secure investments and other concessions promised by U.S.-backed credit institutions and multinationals, the Colombian government will surrender another piece of its autonomy, despite the wishes of its citizens. Democracy in action.

At any rate, after a few days in Bogotá we decided to go south into coffee country to visit some of the plantations and *minifundios* where this crop was grown. Coffee, by the way, is Colombia's largest commodity export, while the United States leads the world in coffee consumption. As we drove through lush green hills we saw the red beans coloring the landscape like Christmas holly. Stopping at a small farm or *minifundio*, we watched the process of drying and discussed production with one of the foremen.

Coffee production

Coffee is the most labor-intensive of all agricultural products. Unlike the well-fed and easy-going Juan Valdéz of the TV commercials, the average coffee laborer is likely to be a bit underweight, subject to stress, overworked, and grossly underpaid.

Coffee (probably from Kaffa, Ethiopia where the plant was first discovered) really refers to the seeds or pods which are found inside the cherry-like fruit of an evergreen shrub of the family *Rubiaceae*, or to the beverage prepared by infusion of those seeds. There are several species of coffee, of which *Coffea arabica, C. liberica,* and *C. robusta* are the most important. The most common in Colombia, Mexico, and Central America is *arabica* (of which there are 12 separate species) and *robusta* (seven varieties). C. *arabica* has a resemblance to a shrub rather than a tree and, although it can grow to a height of 20 feet, is usually kept trimmed to about 10 to 12 feet to allow for easier picking.

The cultivation of coffee is restricted to areas that have a medium average annual temperature of about 70 F. with no highs above 80 F. and no lows below 55 F. It requires a soil that is rich, loose and best composed of mold, disintegrated volcanic rock, and organic matter. It can grow at altitudes up to about 6,000 feet, although *arabica* grows best at about 2,000 feet. The period between planting and harvesting the first crop varies from three to seven years. The best types of commercial coffee are found in Colombia, Brazil, Costa Rica, Guatemala, Mexico, Nicaragua, Haiti and Java. Over the past decade, African coffees, which are cheaper in price but also in quality, have begun invading the U.S. market. They are not relevant here except insofar as their consumption in the U.S. has and continues to affect demand, and thus wages in Latin America, as the U.S. palate becomes conditioned by the coffee importers to accept a more bitter and less robust coffee to replace the fine *arabica* of Latin America.

Labor Intensive

But back to Juan Valdéz and our contemporary coffee worker. When the berries ripen, they must be picked immediately. This means intense labor to get the crop in quickly. Then the coffee berries are thinly spread on a drying pavement, or even on the flat rooftops of the storage sheds and houses of the workers. There, they must be exposed to the sun for three weeks, and turned over constantly by a raker to make sure that they dry uniformly. However, since the harvesting period coincides with the rainy season, additional workers must scurry up to the rooftops at the first sign of rain, rake up all the berries, put them in sacks, store them, and then when the sun returns, climb back up on the roofs, spread out the berries again, and allow them to commence drying. Sometimes the workers must leave off their picking twice in the same day to attend to this urgent demand of the drying berries.

After the three-week drying cycle is complete, the berries are ready for hulling in a de-pulping machine. Then the beans are washed and treated to remove sugars and tannic acid. After cleaning, the coffee is classified by hand (sometimes by machine on larger plantations) into six different sizes, then graded and packed into sacks usually holding 60 kg. or about 132 pounds. This green coffee is then roasted in large revolving cylinders which must be supervised by master roasters. A mistake at this stage, especially too long a time in the roaster, can ruin an entire batch of coffee.

Samples of the various grades are taken from the roaster, brewed and then tasted by experts to determine their quality in the cup. Depending on the country and the area, these have different names which generally signify soft (very fine), hard (standard) and *rioy* (least desirable). Most of the quality coffee exported from the Americas in the past has been the *arabica* form. However, rather than allow the producers to complete the process, which involves grinding the beans, producing the extracts, and mixing them with dextrose or maltose for solubility, U.S. coffee importers have positioned themselves in the economy so that only raw beans are exported. As a result, only 5% of the price the U.S. consumer pays for his coffee actually goes into the wages of the workers who produce it. The percentage is even lower for the coffee worker in Guatemala.

Guatemala

In Guatemala where workers are paid by the pound and coffee yields are much lower than in Colombia, the average picker might average about 200 pounds a day. At about 2½ cents per pound, the worker takes home about $5.00, but often the yields are lower. In terms of percentage of final price, the *altiplano* worker in Guatemala receives about 1% of the price the U.S. consumer pays for the product. Since the initiation of free trade policies and globalization, the situation has worsened for the Guatemalan coffee worker. Previously workers on a plantation were guaranteed housing, clean water, minimum wage, and local education for their children. In addition, a plot of land was usually set aside where a worker and his family could plant vegetables for their own consumption. All that changed with the advent of free trade and globalization. Agribusiness owners forced to impose efficiencies to maximize dwindling profits and pressured by the need for cost-saving if they were to survive, found that hiring seasonal workers relieved them of costly social responsibilities and lowered the price of labor. Moreover, when the picking season was over, the release of these workers put a downward pressure on the labor market, allowing other businesses to contract some of these workers for lower wages. That those who were unable to find employment would be without homes, without medical care or schooling for their children, was not the responsibility of the owners. Nor could the State pick up the slack because with the servicing of loans and the "structural adjustment" package imposed by the IMF as a prerequisite for those loans, funds for social services, education and housing had been drastically cut, as had subsidies for basic foods. The unemployment rate in Guatemala City, which some have speculated is about 40%, has made the city dangerous, and in certain areas unlivable, as groups of angry young men lounge at street corners, intimidate passersby, and engage in random robberies and assaults.

Not long ago I went to the *tianguis* or public market in Guatemala City. I was accompanied by a local businessman and his chauffeur/bodyguard. The bodyguard was an ex-federal policeman, about 6 feet tall and 200 pounds. He also carried a 44 magnum pistol. As we parked on a street near the *tianguis*, he opened the glove compartment and put his pistol and his wallet inside, and suggested that I do the same with my wallet, retaining only a handful of *quetzales* to spend at the market.

When I asked him why he did not want to take his gun into the market he explained: "It's too dangerous. The young thieves will surround you in groups of five or six and, before you know it, they'll have your gun."

This is the reason that guards are not armed in U.S. prisons. There are armed sentries in the guard towers, of course. But inside the cellblocks, guards are outnumbered and guns could easily be taken from even the toughest correctional officer when surrounded and overwhelmed by a dozen convicts. And the comparison of downtown

Guatemala with a maximum security prison where the inmates have taken over, is not totally off the mark. New restraints on the Guatemalan military, a small police force, overcrowded jails, massive unemployment and cutbacks in basic commodities have resulted in a city where the homeless, the hungry, and gangs of delinquents have overwhelmed the city, intimidating whoever they can, whenever they can, wherever they can. One does not see beggars, who used to be so common in poor countries, asking for change or a handout. Today there are young men anxious and willing to work, but finding nothing. Angry, hungry, many with families to support, they've taken to the street and will do whatever they need to do in order to get rice and beans to carry their children through the next day. One does not walk freely in downtown Guatemala City after dark; one does not walk comfortably in many parts of the city even during daylight.

While prices of imports have continued to rise in Guatemala, the price of coffee has fallen, in spite of the fact that there is an International Coffee Agreement to stabilize prices. Part of the reason for the downward pressure is that two multinationals have a virtual monopoly on the purchase of coffee beans; another is the fact that coffee producers are paying for tractors and other equipment with devalued currency, which means that they are investing more real dollars for a smaller return on their investment. While 200 sacks of coffee would have bought a car four years ago, now the same landowner will need to produce 250 sacks. Needless to say, the landowner is not going to do without the car. He might do without the tractor, however, if he can hire sufficient *altiplano* Indians to do the same work of cultivation at less than the cost of gasoline and maintenance.

The low cost of imported coffee results in higher profits for the company and a better return for investors in the U.S. and elsewhere. However, the lower the cost of coffee, the less food the worker can afford to buy for his family. While this might not seem to be of any concern to the investor, it will ultimately affect his well being, too. The U.S. relies on developing countries to dispose of their surpluses in wheat and corn. Nearly 15% of the U.S. gross domestic product is exported with 45% of this going to developing countries. The sustainability of this system is in jeopardy when, as we seen in countries like Guatemala, fewer and fewer people have the resources to buy imported flour or corn, and the government is prohibited by IMF belt-tightening strictures from buying it for them. Exports of other consumer goods such as soft drinks and snack foods are increasingly dependent on the Latin American markets. Coca Cola has higher sales in Mexico, for example, than in the United States. Continued profits and expansion of the stock market depend upon these consumers buying more, not less. And here is the flaw in the system. As countries around the world continue to become more and more dependent on export sales to sustain their economies and attempt to maintain trade surpluses, the market for these products will continue to shrink because the majority of those who would be consumers of these products are less and less able to afford them. This is the worm in the apple of free trade.

Coffee is a perfect example of a micro-economy which clearly reflects the contradictions of free trade and globalization. More jobs are created in the importation, processing, taxing, packaging, advertising, and retailing of coffee than exist for planting, cultivating, growing, harvesting and exporting it. More income is generated in the United States and more jobs because of coffee, than in Guatemala, Mexico, Colombia, El Salvador, Nicaragua and Costa Rica combined. The high school girl selling you the cup of cappuccino at the local coffee bar makes more in one hour than the man who planted, cultivated, and harvested it makes in a day.

What I am talking about here is not just income disparity, or fair wages. Those things, of course, mean nothing to the current economic model. What I am talking about is that the unequal distribution of resources will have serious hemispheric consequences, some of which began in the year 2001, continued sporadically throughout the decade, and culminated in the major recession of 2008. Nor will the Federal Reserve tinkering with the interest rates or other short-term adjustments correct the problem. The problem is endemic to the system. While in the short run depriving the exporter of a product a fair return may result in large profits for the importer, failure to return a fair portion of those profits to the exporter (and the worker) will result in loss of markets for the importer when he exports his products. The reason? Even though the need for the product may exist, there is not sufficient income in the now-importing country with which to buy those goods. Supply far outruns demand which means, ultimately, a recession. The recession will continue unless there are major adjustments in the system.

"Every man's death diminishes me…Ask not for whom the bell tolls; it tolls for thee," wrote John Donne 300 years ago. Most of us read those lines as if they were part of some idealistic spiritual vision. Very nice, but irrelevant in the real world. Most businessmen and most investors have been more concerned with their investments and profits. What happened to Juan Valdéz in Colombia or some *altiplano* Indian in Guatemala seemed of little relevance.

Now we begin to see that this was a kind of blindness induced by greed. We failed to see that globalization can only work if there is fair trade, not free trade. If the Latin American worker gets a fair price for his labor, then he is able to pay a fair price for the grain we export, for the refrigerators we want to sell him, for the cars we'd like him to buy. If he does not, then our only market will be a small oligarchy which will have more and more limited demands. How many refrigerators can a few houses use? Meanwhile, Latin American governments that will increasingly export the cheapest commodity they produce, their own people, and they will import the only commodities they desperately need, helicopters, armored vehicles, and riot control weapons to control the desperate citizens who remain behind.

CHAPTER IV: NICARAGUA YESTERDAY

It seems to me that states, like human beings, are subject to the laws of evolution. Humans begin their lives highly individualized, selfish, and dependent; concerned only with themselves but requiring the good will of others to survive. As Freud so tersely defined the infant, "His Majesty, the child," evolving states, like infants, are solipsistic. This stage of development is followed by a period of protected growth, a developing awareness of the rights, demands and prerogatives of others, a willingness to make concessions, to be socialized. With this comes education, growth of character and "culturalization" which includes not only the traditions inherited by the individual and his family, but the cultures of other tribes and families.

Then comes adolescence, when the individual asserts himself in a different way; this time with a maturity denied the child, but nevertheless with an immaturity obviated by lack of experience in the real world. The adolescent with his new independence seeks domination over others in sports, in scholastic competitions, in school yard bullying, by association with an in-group of peers, or by rejecting the patterns of those around him and assuming a rebellious or artistic pose. Finally, comes maturity in which the individual expands his horizons, accumulates wealth, and competes for salary, commissions, territories, so that he can secure prosperity. Then, the individual chooses a mate, has children and begins a phase wherein he contributes to the welfare of others who are not able to take care of themselves. As the individual grows as a parent, he comes to see in his family the model of a larger society and, conversely, sees society as an extended version of his family.

Societies develop in analogous ways. They begin with the collective will of a strong group with the intention of securing the safety, prosperity and growth of its members. As the state evolves it comes to recognize the need for making concessions to the rights of others not of that group and, in the process of doing so, finds that its own culture is enriched. A state usually passes through a dependent phase, an independent phase, a totalitarian phase, an expansionist phase, a socialistic phase, and, finally, ends up with a collective sense of its being and its relationship to the rest of the world. To use the United States as an example, the colonial period would be its infancy in which it was dependent but protected, allowed to grow and develop with a minimum of interference. Its independence phase was just prior to the Revolutionary War, ending with War of 1812. From that time though the early part of the 20th century the United States was both expansionistic and totalitarian. It was expansionistic, conquering territories in Mexico, the Philippines, Cuba, Santo Domingo, and the

Virgin Islands, and buying other large tracts of land including the Louisiana Territory, Oregon Territory and Alaska. It was totalitarian, systematically exterminating or marginalizing indigenous people in its immediate land mass, and conquering or absorbing other peoples in its far-flung new possessions, while imposing upon them its own laws and customs.

Next, the United States passed through a period of socialism (commencing with President Roosevelt's New Deal in the 1930s) in which it began to realize its obligations to the many that were poor, dispossessed, unemployed and elderly. Subsequent regimes extended this philosophy abroad with the Marshall Plan, the OAS, the Peace Corps, and other initiatives which sought to raise standards of living throughout the world.

The model is reductive, of course. In fact, any nation state is often passing through one or more of these phases simultaneously. Alternatively, while a nation state may be progressing in one area, it may be regressing in another. (An example might be Teddy Roosevelt's limitation on monopolies and trust domestically, while pursuing imperialist interests internationally.) Nevertheless, the model serves generally to describe how nations develop, or (as is the point of this essay), how some nations fail to develop and become moribund, retrograde, or devolved.

It goes without saying that a child whose development is checked by disease, by malnutrition, by abuse and violence will have a stunted adolescence. Likewise the adolescent who is kept dependent and servile and who is manhandled by a variety of surrogate "parents" will not develop into a mature adult. The same may be said of nation states that have been analogously treated.

Take, for example, Nicaragua. Rather than passing cleanly from its dependence stage as a part of the Spanish colonial empire to its independence stage, it was absorbed into the Captaincy General of Guatemala which included Chiapas, El Salvador, Nicaragua, Honduras, Costa Rica, and Mosquita. Its two parents were Spain and Great Britain. Then, under Agustín de Iturbide, Emperor of Mexico, another parent claimed the infant. The bewildered and rebellious child attempted to go out on its own, found that it could not, associated itself with other children (years of confederation with El Salvador and Honduras), engaged in civil war (1821-25), followed by an attempt at "independence" (1825-45), then a new Confederation (Nicaragua, Honduras and El Salvador in 1845), intervention by a less-than-benign stepfather, then the dissolution of the Confederation in 1853.[1]

After that came years of disputes with Great Britain, intervention by U.S. investors trying to insure control of the Isthmus (then a viable alternative to the prospective Panama Canal site), rivalry between the U.S. and Great Britain for control—a kind of custody battle, if you will. This was followed by the invasion and temporary conquest (1855-57) by the U.S. pirate William Walker to whose behavior the U.S. turned a blind eye. What about economic progress, what about intellectual and cultural growth, what about the evolution of democratic institutions, the development of industry, a middle class? What about the country's adolescent stage? Well, coffee growing was introduced and families with large tracts of lands began to prosper. The United Fruit Company had large plantations of bananas for export abroad. Some railroads were built, but most commerce was dominated by the United States, with its Marines present to ensure the election of officials who would grant the U.S. rights in perpetuity to construct a canal via the San Juan River and Lake Nicaragua, as well as a ninety-nine year lease on a naval base on the Gulf of Fonseca. One of the most famous poets of all Latin America, Rubén Dario (1867-1916), was born in Nicaragua but spent most of his life in Costa Rica and in Europe

Does Nicaragua sound like a place you'd like to live at this point? To return to the developmental model: this is not a neglected child; this is an abused and exploited child. Its beauty and its health are being sold to the highest bidder. As a nation, its natural resources are not being developed, its children are not being educated, and there is not an inkling of a democratic institution. There is essentially no middle class, culture is expropriated as soon as it is developed, and the best and brightest either leave the country or are destroyed by government forces in league with the U.S. Marines, who are effectively operating as strong-arm enforcers for the exploiters.[2]

In 1925 when a successful revolution attempted to move the established families to share the power and afford some relief to the poor, the U.S. refused to recognize the new government and landed Marines to mandate a new election. In 1931, the Sandino Revolution, a people's movement to establish universal education, land reform and distribution of wealth, again offered hope to the repressed people. Augusto César Sandino led the peasants in their fight for equitable distribution of land. But machetes and grenades made from "sardine tins filled with stones"[3] could not overcome the Springfield rifles and Gatling guns of the National Guard and the U.S. Marines. Still, they were sufficient to bring the dictatorial government to the bargaining table. After three years of guerrilla warfare Sandino and his troops agreed to the government's request for a cease-fire. Sandino went to Managua to meet with the Nicaraguan president and was assassinated en route. His self-confessed murderer was General Anastasio Somoza who later stated that U.S. ambassador Arthur Bliss Lane had given the order for the assassination. General Somoza himself would assume the presidency as well as forty-six coffee plantations and fifty-one cattle ranches, his reward for being a good steward for his U.S. masters.

Somoza, his sons and a handful of other families would "rule" Nicaragua for the next forty-six years, with the U.S. military aiding and abetting the suppression of any liberal forces. For all this period and well into the present, the Roman Catholic Church shamelessly condoned the brutalization of this nation. When individual priests (and, on one occasion, a bishop) stood up for the poor and oppressed, they were jailed, tortured and murdered, until, under Pope John Paul II, a conservative hierarchy was appointed to ensure that such embarrassments would not recur.

In 1974, General Anastasio Somoza (son of the earlier eponymous Somoza) declared martial law in an attempt to control the Sandinista rebels (named after 1930s land reformer and liberal leader Augusto César Sandino). Repression in the country grew as Somoza tried to hold on to his power through terror and repression. By 1978 violent opposition to his regime had spread to almost all the classes, and nationwide strikes against the government touched off a civil war which ended with the flight of Somoza in July, 1979 to Paraguay where he was assassinated a year later.[4]

The Sandinista Revolution, led by Daniel Ortega, instituted agrarian reform, wrested control of the banks from foreigners, prevented Somoza's forces from recruiting Miskito Indians, inaugurated an art museum with over three hundred works of international stature, established "Literacy Brigades"[5] (the largest and most successful literacy program in the history of the country), opened dozens of free medical clinics, created community-oriented shopping centers, subsidized publishing houses (most notably *Nueva Nicaragua*) to bring out inexpensive paperbacks which were distributed even in the remote parts of the country. Revolutionary workers re-paved hundreds of kilometers of roads destroyed by earthquakes and shelling, and they developed the first viable system of public transportation. All this despite the fact that the United States countered the internal progress with an economic blockade, including the freezing of credits. And, despite the fact that there was mass capital flight, as the wealthiest families sent their money and their sons to Miami, while the average Nicaraguan lived in fear of the next attack by U.S.-backed "Contras" to restore Potomac-style "democracy".

Although Denmark, Mexico, UNESCO and Cuba helped with needed economic aid, much of it was drained by the constant necessity to defend the borders against Contra aggression.[6] But the revolution was truly a popular one. It was not merely Daniel Ortega and his combatants; it was poets and intellectuals such as Ernesto Cardenal, Sergio Ramírez and Tomás Borges. It was housewives and farmers, teachers and bureaucrats. It was formerly passive people, lacking even the most elementary tools, rising up in dynamic participation and community action. "People are more disposed to suffer when the evils are sufferable," wrote Thomas Jefferson, "than to change those things to which they have long been accustomed." But there comes a time, as it did for Jefferson and the U.S. colonists in 1776, when the evils become insufferable. Now, after forty-nine years of oppression, of no voice in how they were governed, of daily repression and fear, the people of Nicaragua took power the only way they knew; by force. The issue was popular sovereignty, nationalism, people controlling their own destiny. The issue (to re-claim a word grown old with the lichen of lies and betrayals) was "democratic rule." However, the United States continued to back anti-Sandinista Contra forces, and in 1985 the U.S.

House authorized massive military aid to ensure their success against the legitimate Nicaraguan government. The subsequent diversion of additional funds to the Contras from secret arms sales to Iran, which received massive press coverage, was to cause a major scandal in the U.S. However, the destruction of the Sandinista revolution, the last best hope for the people of Nicaragua, rated barely a paragraph in the *New York Times*.

In 1990, after a decade of struggle, the Sandinistas were unable to mount an effective election campaign and lost to a compromise candidate, Violeta Chamorro, whose husband was a victim of civil violence. The Sandinista leader, Daniel Ortega, would go on to become an "entrepreneur" who by his actions and his deeds betrayed the revolution, turned free clinics into for-profit enterprises, and converted confiscated property into private holdings. The results were thousands dead, the best hope of true democratic reform stillborn, and Nicaraguan government more than ever dependent on good relations with the United States to maintain its economic survival. The words of Latin American historian Eduardo Galeano best sum up the tragic results:

> Nicaragua was sentenced to ten years of war in the 1980s when it committed the insolence of being Nicaragua. An army recruited, trained, armed and led by the United States tormented the country, while a campaign to poison world opinion portrayed the Sandinista revolution as a conspiracy hatched in the basement of the Kremlin. Nicaragua wasn't attacked because it was a satellite of a great power but to force it into being one. Nicaragua wasn't attacked because it lacked

democracy but so that democracy would be lacking. While fighting the war, the Sandinistas also taught half a million people to read and write, cut infant mortality by a third, and inspired a sense of solidarity and a yearning for justice in many, many people. That was their challenge and that was their damnation. In the end, exhaustion from the long devastating war cost the Sandinistas an election. And later, as tends to happen, several of their leaders sinned against hope by disowning their own words and deeds in an astonishing about-face.[8]

Notes for NICARAGUA YESTERDAY

1. The early history of Nicaragua is gleaned from many sources which I consulted along the way. A brief overview is available from the well-known text edited by A. Curtis Wilgus and Raul d'Ecu, *Latin American History*. 5th Ed. Barnes & Noble. New York, 1969 at pp. 196-203.

2. Celso Furtado. *The Development of Underdevelopment*. The University of California Press. Berkeley, 1970.

3. The references to Sandino and the grenades made from sardine tins comes from Eduardo Galeano's *Open Veins of Latin America: Five Centuries of the Pillage of A Continent.* Trans. Cedric Belfrage, with an introduction by Isabel Allende. Monthly Review Press. New York, 1997. (25th Anniversary Edition with additions from the original of 1973), pp. 110-111.

4. Some of the material for the onset and later development of the Sandinista revolution comes from contemporary periodicals including *The Wall Street Journal* and *La Prensa*. Other material is from *Los Sandinistas* by Gabriel García Márquez, et al. La Oveja Negra. Bogotá, 1979.

5. Information about the Literacy Brigades, the subsidized publishing houses and other positive results of the revolution comes from *Nicaraguan Sketches* by Julio Cortázar. Trans. by Kathleen Weaver. W.W. Norton and Co. New York, 1989. Cortázar received the Ruben Dario Award in 1983. Although an Argentine, he made many visits to Nicaragua both before and during the conflict. He is considered one of the most trustworthy sources of information on the revolution. See also Gabriel García Márquez, "El argentino que se hizo querer de todos," *Casa de las Americas*. Nos. 145-46 (July-August, 1984), p. 23.

6.The support of Denmark and other countries for the revolution is also from Cortázar book.

7. For Márquez' support of the Sandinista cause, see note #4.

8. The final quote is from Eduardo Galeano's polemical work *Upside Down: A Primer For The Looking Glass World.* Trans. by Mark Fried. Henry Holt & Co. New York, 2000, p. 214.

CHAPTER V: NICARAGUA TODAY

"So, would you want to live there?" I asked somewhat facetiously in the preceding chapter. Well, many people do for a variety of reasons, including U.S. expatriates who come to visit and end up staying. Let me list a few of the positive aspects of Nicaragua so that you may have a clearer view of the country, separated from its troubled history.

1. Nicaragua is the largest country in Central America, with the smallest population. This means a more relaxed pace of life, a quieter lifestyle. Traffic is modest even in the largest cities, and parks and historic places are untrammeled by crowds of tourists.

2. The clear waters and sandy beaches of the Caribbean are lined with coral reefs which are home to countless species of tropical fish, and hundreds of sunken ships. One can spend hours snorkeling and skin diving. On the Pacific coast one can walk along the beach for miles in relative peace and solitude, or ride—as I did—on one of the country's many pure Arabian horses along the strand. Near the capital is a lake so huge it contains hundreds of archipelagos and large islands that you can visit by motor launch.

3. The people are quiet and formally polite. Because of centuries of mixed marriages, there is no racial prejudice. Many Nicaraguans are part *indio*, part black, part European and have a high level of tolerance for other cultures and foreigners. Moreover, despite years of U.S. interventions, there is little in the way of anti-U.S. feeling. Most Nicaraguans are able to distinguish between the policies of a government and the nature of its people.

4. While the lowlands and beaches are often hot and somewhat humid all year long, there are mountain resorts and cool, cloud-covered forests; there are also lush national parks and volcanoes. The country is so heavily wooded that the air is constantly recycled, making its air the healthiest in the hemisphere. Even Managua, a city of more than half a million, has more trees per block than any city in the world.

5. An important tobacco and coffee exporter, it produces cigars that easily rival the Cuban "Habana," and varieties of coffee that are rich, full-bodied and mellow. And, while its cultural landmarks (including its Museum of Art and its baroque Metropolitan Cathedral) have suffered from earthquakes, civil war, and government neglect, there are still fascinating local museums, a National Theater, a Cultural Palace and an excellent university.[1]

I was invited to Nicaragua in the fall of 2001, just prior to the elections, to present a talk to teachers at a Central American conference for the Tri-Association of American Schools. I also spent some days there visiting with old friends, touring the city, driving in the mountains, eating good food, relaxing at the beach.

"But, is it safe?" is one of the first questions North Americans tend to ask whenever one returns from visiting a nation which has been at war. The answer is always comparative.

The beach resorts are safe enough, fenced-off, and patrolled by security guards. The historic center of the city, mostly empty of visitors when we were there, was quiet, with occasional youngsters (all under ten years of age) asking for handouts. There are teenage gangs which scoot in and out of traffic stealing purses and infest the large markets. There are also land mines, left behind by the Contras and the Marines, which lie hidden in the hills and the woods. But neither the city nor the countryside *feels* dangerous in the sense that say, Detroit or Guatemala City does to the casual visitor. Perhaps this is because the numbers of delinquents is so small, and the respectable population and the police comfortably outnumber them. That, of course, will change unless steps are taken now.

Primary education reaches only a small portion of the population. Illiteracy rates are at 40% and climbing. The average age of Nicaraguans is 18 (the voting age is 16!); it is a very young country with many of its intellectuals, its moral leaders and teachers dead from civil war, in temporary exile, or permanently emigrated to Costa Rica or the U.S. The foreigners who have come to live there are a mixed breed. Some are Japanese farmers who have come because of the cheap land. Some are former Marines and consular workers who have married locals and retired there. Others are Christian missionaries, mostly Protestant Evangelicals who have come to fill the gap left by the dismissal of liberal Catholic bishops and priests. Others are teachers, North American and Danish, who have come to work in the schools.

One of my friends, Brian Sullivan, who had worked as a teacher at the American School in Managua for six years, spoke to me of the frustrations. "The best students leave the country as soon as they are able. They go to the U.S. or Canada, or to Costa Rica, and they seldom return. These are the young people who could be the new leaders of Nicaragua, but there is little here to keep them."[2] According to the local police, many other adolescents with less education or skills also leave the country. Up north, they work at menial jobs as illegal aliens, join gangs in L.A. or Phoenix, are caught by the police or immigration authorities and are deported to Nicaragua as hardened delinquents who roam alleys and streets preying on unwary residents and tourists, or they fight among themselves in barrios which are the enclaves of local gang lords. In the words of Eduardo Galeano:

> In the seventies and eighties, years of revolution and war, young people saw themselves in their country, in the colony that wanted to become a country, but the youth of the nineties were left without a mirror. Now they are patriots of the barrio, and they fight to the death against gangs or enemy blocks. By defending their territory and organizing themselves to fight and steal, they feel a little less alone and a little less poor in their atomized and impoverished world. They share what they steal

and spend the loot from muggings on glue, marijuana, drink, bullets, knives, Nike shoes and baseball caps.[3]

In 1990 when the Nicaragua electorate, tired of war, weary of occupation by U.S. and Contra troops, voted for a pro-U.S. president, the United States promised massive aid to help rebuild the country; they promised debt forgiveness, economic incentives, and prosperity. Nothing materialized. The U.S. packed up its advisors and left a shattered capital, a scarred and pitted countryside, and an unknown number of land mines behind, as well as a mined harbor. The United States abandoned the country which had been bled dry of its resources, deprived by death or emigration of some of its best and brightest, with the rest left mired in poverty, unemployment and random violence.

I arrived in the fall of 2001 and spent part of my time at the Hotel InterContinental in a room which looked out on a destitute barrio, a jumble of dirt paths and tumbled-together shacks without running water on one side, and a modern conference center and shopping plaza on the other. There were power outages at least once a day and if the hotel had a generator, it apparently was not working. This was one of Managua's five star hotels. The conference center was well-appointed and of the quality one would expect in any large city in the U.S. or Europe. The facilities were modern and up-to-date and the staff polite and efficient. Since electric outages generally occurred in late afternoon when most city residents returned home, we had no problem with power at our events.

The shopping center was a bit bleaker, reminiscent of Eastern Europe in the seventies, or one of those failing, off-the-beaten-track shopping centers in a declining inner-city. There were few products available in the drug store; much of the stock was dusty. Cheap U.S. plastic toys overflowed the aisles of one store; CD's were jammed into another while a stereo played music so loud it made the windows vibrate. Polyester clothes were casually displayed in one boutique; costume jewelry in other stores. When I asked my friend Sullivan about the scarcity of quality goods, he said, "People who can afford those things go to Mexico City or Miami to buy them." This was one of those proletarian shopping centers, I supposed. One of the products of the failed revolution. But then, the Sandinistas opened publishing houses, produced cheap paperbacks. So, I asked, "Why no bookstore?" A Nicaraguan teacher who had joined us replied, "No one reads." He shrugged his shoulders resignedly. "That's the problem, or at least one of the problems."

Later we walked out, and down the street past a disco which was iron-barred and screened by palm trees from the barrio I'd seen earlier from the window of the hotel room. We walked past the barrio where children of primary school age were playing soccer in the street. We watched them play for a while, and then one boy about twelve years old came over and asked for change so that he could buy a *refresco*. We gave it to him, and asked why he was not in school. "No clothes for school, *maestro*," he said unabashed, gesturing elegantly to his ragged short pants, his naked feet. Behind him, on one of the dirt paths that rose up the hill to where the wooden shacks of the barrio were precariously balanced, a young soldier watched us. He shifted his automatic rifle upon his shoulder. I waved to him to let him know that we were harmless and not about to molest the children. He nodded solemnly. Then, he turned to wistfully watch a teenage girl walk down the path and onto the road. When she disappeared from view, he cast one last look at us below, and then ducked under a collapsing porch roof to get out of the blazing sun.

The election was coming up and we talked of that. The two candidates were Daniel Ortega and Enrique Bolaños. Ortega was the former leader of the Sandinistas who after ten years had conceded defeat to Violeta Chamorro in the first free election in modern times, a result of the democracy Ortega helped bring about during his finest hour. But the young idealist of the eighties was not the Ortega running today. Now he is a shady businessman who has installed some of his loyal followers in privatized industries and ranches hidden behind Panamanian corporate fronts. He lives in a mansion surrounded by eight foot walls and manned guard towers. The intellectuals who once supported him such as Ernesto and Fernando Cardenal, Gioconda Belli, and María Téllez have long since deserted him and the party.

His opponent is a former Contra, friend and ally of the current president Arnoldo Alemán, whose outright corruption and political patronage is well-known. Alemán is a friend to the United States and has actively supported the Washington Consensus. He squeezed his country to pay off $6 billion in debt, eliminating most social services, opening up low wage U.S.-owned *maquiladora* plants, and in the process skimmed off enough to increase his personal wealth to an astronomical $250 million with three properties and two heliports in one of the poorest nations in the world.[4]

The campaign is something of a joke. Daniel Ortega, because of his past history as a populist leader, his youthful appearance, and his familiarity with music and popular culture, easily has more than half of the predicted vote. Bolaños, a 73 year-old reactionary who cares little for the people and less for social movements, nevertheless makes an effort to campaign. Few really take him seriously. Marc Cooper writing for *Mother Jones* magazine describes a typical election rally:

> At the staging point, party officials in pressed chinos, polo shirts and Ray-Bans busily organized the motorcade. Street gangs, replete with tattoos and bandanas, were hired to fill the marshaled pickup trucks and wave party flags. As the motorcade wound through the dank industrial barrios, sidewalk onlookers jeered and laughed. The caravan arrived at the nearly deserted Calendaria Park, where another rent-a-crowd of impoverished Nicaraguans was packed into a school bus. Party officials brought a single Winnie the Pooh piñata to lure local families out of their dirt-floored shacks. When Bolaños showed

up, the crowd was brought in to cheer him. Standing on the back of a sound truck, the candidate shouted a series of verbal jabs. His message was simple: Me—or the Sandinistas.

Ultimately, it was no contest. Although Bolaños could only claim 30% of the electorate in September, after the terrorist attack on the twin towers in the United States on September 11th the contest had suddenly changed. The United States let it be known that if Daniel Ortega and the Sandinista Party were elected, it would seriously consider declaring Nicaragua a terrorist state. Frightened at such a prospect, the people rushed to the polls. With less than 20% of the votes counted, Daniel Ortega conceded the election.[6]

The new election almost certainly guarantees several things. There will be no more confiscations of private estates; those who have them will keep what they have, no matter how ill-gotten their gains. There will be no prosecutions for fraud for any former officials or friends of the outgoing president. Nicaragua will continue its austerity program to pay off its foreign loans. The budget for social services will drop even below its pre-Sandinista levels. More funding will go to the police and military, not to stop street gangs and delinquency, but (as has been recently shown) to bludgeon university students protesting lower fares for public transportation. Education will stagnate under this "business friendly" and "austere" government, and poverty, in the words of sociologist Orlando Nuñez, will turn "into raw hunger."[7]

Seventy-five percent of the Nicaraguan population now survives on less than $2 a day. The average wage for someone with stable employment is $150 a month. Approximately 40% of the population is illiterate (the rate for women is close to 60%), and over 600,000 Nicaraguans are suffering from malnutrition.[8] That those figures will worsen is unquestioned even by the most optimistic analysts, since the newly elected president has neither the social conscience nor the will to improve them.

To return to my earlier analogy of evolution, Nicaragua has been bombed, bled, earthquaked, mined, evacuated and despoiled. Its people have been shot, starved, or have fled to other nations for safety. It has devolved and regressed to a stage that is far worse than in the most difficult days of the Sandinista revolution when at least it had solidarity, hope, a vibrant popular culture, full employment of human resources, a sense of mission for its young people, a safety net for its elderly, a spiritual sense of itself as a people.[9]

Nicaragua is not looking ten years into the future for that vibrant socialistic stage which characterized the best of our New Deal under President Roosevelt: when art and public works, when the WPA and Conservation Corps and a sense of mission fired the people of the U.S. Nicaragua is now a hundred years from that stage. It needs to train intelligent young men and women to take up the mantle of leadership. But most of those young men and women have left, along with the teachers and professors who could train them. The country needs to educate its children for the next generation but most of those children are poorly clothed, weakened by malnutrition and unable to attend schools even if the schools existed—and they do not. It needs institutions which can inspire respect and confidence but the Church, like the ruins of the bulldozed Cathedral destroyed by the earthquake of 1972, is a mere façade, while the government is corrupt and arrogant in its impregnability. The United States, which could be Nicaragua's friend and ally, is more concerned with the bottom line of short-term investment and has abandoned moral authority and practical assistance for short-sighted political expediency.

John F. Kennedy was fond of quoting the story of the great French Marshall Lyautey who asked his gardener to plant a tree. The gardener objected that the tree was slow-growing and would not reach maturity for a hundred years. The Marshall replied, "In that case, there is no time to lose. Plant it this afternoon."[10] There is no time to lose in Nicaragua. Tomorrow could be too late.

Managua—September, 2001.

Nicaragua Update, September 2009

I returned to Nicaragua in 2009 for a brief visit. One of the most remarkable occurrences since I was last there was the November 2006 election of Daniel Ortega and his Sandinista coalition, in spite of Washington's pressures and threats to stop the flow of remittances from Nicaraguans living abroad. Mark Engler, writing in *The Nation,* noted that U.S. Ambassador Paul Trivielli, "violating diplomatic protocol..." expressed an "open preference for Ortega's opponents."[11] It took a great deal of courage on the part of the Nicaraguan electorate to stand up to such pressures and to vote for a change after sixteen years of conservative government and economic "belt tightening" (Newspeak conservative euphemism for slow starvation).

The revised version of Daniel Ortega is no longer the idealistic revolutionary. His pact with the opposition, his accumulation of wealth as a deal-making legislator, have left his image tarnished and his stature diminished. He is also older and, although 64 is not elderly, for someone who has spent seven years in prison, fought in the streets and the hills as a guerrilla leader, and served two terms as president, the years have taken their toll. His speeches are often rambling, contradictory and characterized by repetition and slogans.

On the positive side he has significantly increased his budget for both education and health (2008). He has, with the help of Cuba and Venezuela, opened up two new power generating plants (2007) which will help reduce the energy deficit and limit the blackouts so common to this country. A new water treatment plant is finally completed in Managua, although much of the credit for this must go to his predecessor.

He has also entered into agreements with Iran for development of a deep sea port, for another electrical generating plant, and for a major housing project. His partnership with Hugo Chávez may result in a pipeline to take Venezuelan oil across the isthmus, resulting in increased revenue for both countries. A bit unsettling, however, is the news that, as Chávez has already done in Venezuela, Ortega is exploring ways to ensure his re-election, currently prohibited by the constitution.

Nicaragua is still the second poorest country in the hemisphere (after Haiti) and remains marginal on the geopolitical stage. So despite the Ronald Reagan rhetoric of the eighties which is now being resurrected by some conservatives in Washington, Nicaragua is not a threat to U.S. security. It may be that with a higher standard of living, better education and health care, clean water and electricity, the country could become a decent place to live and work some decades down the road. We'll just have to wait and see. But this time around it is the people of Nicaragua who will decide.

Notes for NICARAGUA TODAY

1. Much of the material in the descriptive section of this chapter is from personal observation. I had the opportunity to stay at a Pacific resort which was the former estate and stronghold of the dictator Somoza. In the morning I rode an Arabian horse from the stables which were confiscated by the Sandinistas, and in the evenings walked the beaches and spoke with fishermen and children. I also took a motor launch across Lake Nicaragua, and spent a day in Granada. I visited Managua's Historic *Centro*: the National Theater, the Cultural Palace, and the ruins of the Metropolitan Cathedral. With some friends I also went to a poor barrio, a local primary school, a *secundaria*, and the American School of Nicaragua. I spoke with several dozen teachers, and attended sessions on the problems associated with teaching in the country. I also spoke with local policemen, several teenagers, a Bolaños supporter, and a former Sandinista. I also spent some time with Evangelical missionaries who were working in the countryside, and attended a conference on land mine removal. Other information on the country was obtained from the Nicaraguan Institute of Tourism. www.intur.gob.ni

2. Interviews with Brian Sullivan in Managua, Nicaragua. Oct. 13-15, 2001.

3. Eduardo Galeano, *Upside Down: A Primer for the Looking Glass World,* p. 216.

4. Most of the information on the pre-election maneuvering, the biographies of the candidates, and the warning from the U.S., was from personal interviews and from *La Prensa* (Oct. 11-17, 2001).

5. The Bolaños rally is wonderfully described in Marc Cooper's article "The Lost Revolution" from *Mother Jones.* Sept./Oct., 2001. pp. 71-77.

6. Ortega's concession to Bolaños with only 20% of the vote in was from the *New York Times Headline Service* (internet) on the evening of the election.

7. United Nations Children's Fund. *The State of the World's Children 2000*. UNICEF. New York, 2000.

8. United Nations Population Fund. *The State of the World's Population 2000*. UNICEF. New York, 2000.

9. Castañeda, Jorge G. *Nicaragua: Contradicciones en la revolución*. Tiempo Extra Editores. México, 1980.

10. The quote from John F. Kennedy is from *The Quotable Mr. Kennedy*. Ed. by Gerald Gardner. Popular Library. New York, 1963.

11. Mark Engler. "The Return of Daniel Ortega" from *The Nation*, November 7, 2006.
http://www.thenation.com/doc/20061120/ortega

CHAPTER VI: GLOBAL VILLAGE OR GATED COMMUNITY?

One thing is for sure: if you want to have political power in the United States, you cannot propose legalization of drugs, or a flexible immigration policy. Senator Dennis DeConcini (D-AZ) discovered the former toward the end of his career as state attorney general when he suggested that decriminalization of drugs was the only intelligent policy for our nation.

He was approached by the spin doctors and told that while decriminalization might be intelligent policy it was not something that could be sold to U.S. voters or to his fellow politicians. He quickly modified his views in time for the U.S. Senate race, and to this writer's knowledge, never raised the matter again.

President George W. Bush discovered similar kinds of pressures from his own party (as well as Democrats) forcing him to backpedal on his accords with Mexican President Vicente Fox for following through with the letter and the spirit of NAFTA and formalized procedures for Mexican workers coming north of the border. Despite Bush's personal belief in a dynamic inter-American economic and immigration policy, he had been told by his advisors to go slow. President Obama now faces those same pressures.

Drugs and immigration are two areas in which "public opinion" has been mobilized by various pressure groups, as well as government policy makers, to essentially polarize the nation and insure that no rational accords will be developed. It is not in the self-interest of the DEA, the FBI, state and local law enforcement, DARE and other Law Enforcement Administration Program recipients to change the current policy on drugs. Nor is it in the interest of the Federal Department of Prisons, state and county departments of corrections and their thousands of employees, to retreat from the present philosophy.

With the USSR out of the picture, mobilization of federal resources, including the armed services, demands that there be some clear and present danger. Threats of not enough oil or too many drugs are acceptable solutions for armed intervention, whether in the Gulf of Persia or the mountains of Colombia.

The immigration policy is, of course, even more complex. Statistics are available on both sides of the question. Arguments can be made which tend to show that, while those in favor of reducing immigration are short-sighted, those in favor of a more open policy are ingenuous. But there is a rational path independent of the rhetoric and the equivocation of partisan-applied statistics.

The New York-based "Project USA" has a "Truthmobile" which goes around the country, appearing at local parades and festivals, putting banners on bridges, warning of the dangers of immigration. Their latest effort is a street-wide banner which reads: "In your 20s? Immigration will double U.S. population in your lifetime." The director of the project based this incendiary statement on the fact that the 2000 census showed the U.S. population as having increased 13.2 percent over the past ten years, despite the fact that women born in the U.S. had a fertility rate of less than two children per capita. Result: the increase in population was due to immigration and the higher birth rates among immigrant mothers, especially Mexicans. He went on to say that the rate of immigration was the highest it has ever been in the history of the United States and that we were selling our birthright, degrading our cities, and destroying our heritage. He was immediately charged with being racist and the argument was mired down in name-calling and rhetoric.

A better approach would be to analyze his figures, determine what increase was a natural one for a developed nation, add that figure to the immigration figure, and that figure to minority births. This was not done. If it had been, we would be able to determine that immigration added less than a third to our population growth over the past ten years.

Rate of Immigration Less Now than 80 Years ago

An even more useful statistic would be not the actual number of immigrants in any given period but the percentage of immigrants. By almost any reasoning or statistical analysis, the rate of immigration is not even close to being as high as it's been percentage-wise in the past. In the 1840s when the population of the U.S. was about 20 million, there were 1,500,000 legal immigrants admitted to the U.S. The following decade, 3,000,000 came to our shores. Most of these immigrants were German and Irish and radically changed our schools, our churches, and our politics, and also created a backlash similar to that experienced by Mexicans today in California.

Between 1860 and 1900 some 14,000,000 immigrants were admitted to the United States, with 18,600,000 arriving between 1900 and 1930. In 1907 alone there were 1,280,000 legal immigrants to the U.S. Given the United States population during the 1900-1930 period, immigration accounted for about 1% of the U.S. population. Given today's population, immigration actually constitutes about .003%. As far as Mexicans are concerned, the IRS estimates that between 100,000 and 200,000 cross the border each year to reside permanently in the

United States. The rest are seasonal workers who return home after the harvests.

While Mexicans might seem to be the most visible of these immigrants, this is largely due to the fact that the U.S. labels people from Guatemala, El Salvador, Nicaragua, Panama, Honduras, Costa Rica, Cuba and Puerto Rico (not to mention all South Americans) as "Latino"—thus effectively substituting for a mélange of diverse cultures and societies, a convenient "racial" envelope. Since Mexico is our closest "Latino" neighbor and the most visible in our news reports, these other immigrants are perceived as being part of the same group. In fact, however, Nicaraguans, Panamanians, Guatemalans and Salvadorans have come to the U.S. as refugees from bloodbaths and government reprisals due to U.S. intervention in those countries. Cubans have come to the United States as part of an ongoing public policy to embarrass Fidel Castro and hasten the end of his government. Puerto Ricans already have citizenship privileges in the United States and need no permits to enter the mainland. "Too many Mexicans" indeed!

The Economic Impact of Immigration

Immigration is one of the bases of economic growth for any nation, but even more particularly for the United States. This is classical economics which even the most conservative analysts accept.

New workers increase the supply of goods and services with their labor, and they also increase demand for goods and services as a result of their wages. This widening circle increases the wealth of all nations but especially the people within the host nation. It has worked very well for the United States over the past two centuries of its existence and will continue to do so. There may be short-term job replacement in low level labor and services industries, but this is more than offset by the new jobs that immigrants create by their own work and earnings. Their spending creates an increase in demand for groceries, housing, clothing, and the businesses which supply those commodities invest their expanding profits in new jobs and machinery. It is the cycle which has led to U.S. economic growth and prosperity.

It is perhaps no accident that the lowest period of immigration in the United States was during the Great Depression. Fear, recession and unemployment provoke anti-immigration movements, and these in turn help put on the brakes which ensure a slowdown of the economy. If anyone doubts the positive impact of Mexicans and Mexican-Americans on the U.S. economy today, I suggest reading the reports of the San Antonio Chamber of Commerce as one of many examples of the millions of dollars that are poured into the U.S. economy by this particular group each year.

Immigration and Welfare

Several years ago the argument could be made that the impact of immigration on social service providers was a financial burden. However, with the welfare reforms of 1996 this objection has not only melted away, it has actually provided some ammunition for the opposition. Undocumented workers in the United States, approximately 3,000,000 of them, pay U.S., state and local taxes both as workers and consumers. They also have social security taxes deducted from their payroll checks, and recover none of the benefits from those payments.

Many Mexican workers return home after a season or two in the fields. The funds taken out of their paychecks by employers end up in the U.S. Treasury, not in the pockets of these workers. Of those who remain, none are eligible to secure unemployment compensation, SSI, or social security retirement, because they are not legal residents. Much is made of the fact the children of these workers use our schools and our emergency medical services and a dollar cost is usually fixed to determine that. However, I have yet to see the dollar value of the payroll taxes, sales taxes, and social security payments of these 3 million undocumented workers deducted from that figure, which would give us the real social cost (or profit, which is more likely) to our nation.

Negative Perception Belies the Reality

Yet, according to a *Newsweek* poll, 60% of U.S. citizens see the current levels of immigration as bad, 59% percent say many immigrants wind up on welfare, and 47% think we should make it more difficult for Latinos to come into the country. What is going on here? Well, the "racist" argument which I mentioned as the knee-jerk response to "Project USA" is quite relevant here.

A *Newsweek* article by Tom Morganthau entitled "America: Still a Melting Pot?" after discussing how the bulk of immigrants to the U.S. are now from Latin America and the Caribbean, states that "upwards of 80% [of immigrants to the U.S.] are persons of color: so much for the myth that U.S. policy is racist." Well, I don't know about the "myths" of U.S. policy but the statement itself is racist. In the 1840s until the time of the Civil War, the Irish, members of the Celtic race, were considered inferior to Anglo-Saxons; a lower breed. Scientific studies were done (including the pseudo-science of phrenology) to show that the Irish were "less evolved as a race than either the Indian or the Negro." It was not until the Civil War, when the North needed them as troops, that the Irish became "white."

Most Latin Americans, except the native peoples and those artists and poets with strong ties to their indigenous cultural roots, consider themselves to be "white" people, and are so considered in other parts of the world. In the U.S., however, they are considered as "people of color" and by the same magazine cited above, as contributors to the "browning of America."

In Mexico one even sees beer commercials which show a young man choosing both the *güera* (the blond girl) and the *"güera"* or light beer. In Colombia and Costa Rica where the native peoples were long ago exterminated by war or disease, there is little question that the citizens are white. Yet, U.S. society persists in these arbitrary classifications: white, black, Hispanic. It is a policy that fosters racism even when it is used in a benevolent way; just as the government funding for "minority" (read "persons of color") projects is demeaning and divisive.

An anthology funded by the National Endowment for the Arts which features the best black writers in the U.S., or the best Chicano writers, or the best woman writers, demeans the art of those included by its very exclusiveness. When the committee in Stockholm gave Toni Morrison the Nobel Prize for Literature they did not give it to her because she was a woman or because she was black. They gave it to her because she was a great writer, the same as Octavio Paz, Seamus Heaney, Joseph Brodsky or Nadine Gordimer.

Racial politics is a part of the U.S. It has always been how we defined ourselves as a people. As late as 1846 when the U.S.

Marines entered the "Halls of Montezuma" to conquer Mexico and take two-fifths of the country, there was so little sense of national unity that the band played three different national anthems: "Hail Columbia," "Yankee Doodle" and the "Star Spangled Banner." U.S. citizens were defined in the 1840s and 1850s not by what they were but by what they were not. A true "American" was not a Negro, an Indian, a Chinaman, or an Irishman. We think we've come a long way in the past 150 years. All of our textbooks paint U.S. history as a series of progressions. The reality is that much of U.S. history is circular, and many of the attitudes and beliefs of our forebears are inscribed in our laws and our culture. Political correctness and diversity notwithstanding, the U.S. remains a nation which expanded its territorial limits and its dominance over the hemisphere not by tolerance of other cultures but by exterminating them (Native Americans), conquering them (Mexicans, Filipinos), enslaving them (African-Americans), or by demonizing them (Irish, Italians).

The richest 1% of the country still owns most of its productive capacity and still calls the shots. Who's up, who's down, who's out and who's in, constitute the "bread and circuses" which the Caesars provide to keep us from thinking too much.

What Happened to Globalization Theory?

The rich nations which praise globalization, liberalism, free markets, free flow of investment and capital, are rejecting their own principles when it come to free flow of labor. One of the reasons that poorer countries are falling further and further behind as a result of globalization and the new economy is the curtailment on freedom of movement. Since the postwar period, rich countries have largely excluded the free flow of labor into their markets. Low-skilled labor is not free to flow across international boundaries in search of more lucrative jobs. While immigration in the U.S. and Europe is certainly significant, it is very small (less than the rate of 70 years ago) compared to the dramatic increases in world population over that period.

Europe and the U.S. together in a given year admit only 0.04 of all potential immigrants. This would not be so critical if wealthier nations were sending capital as well as technologies to developing nations so that growth of poorer economies would be ensured. However, while foreign direct investment increased from 4% to 12% of the world GNP in the past twenty years, little has ended up in the poorer countries. According to Bruce Scott of Harvard, "70 percent went from one rich nation to another, 8 developing countries received 20 percent, and the remainder was divided among more than 100 poor nations." Most of the poorer nations are exporters of agricultural commodities and minerals, and these categories have decreased as a percentage of world trade: from about 70 percent at the start of the century to about 20 percent at present.

Growth in world markets has shifted to manufactured goods, services, and informational technologies. The opening of capital markets in developing countries has merely resulted in takeovers by international firms, draining the raw materials from these nations (reminiscent of the worse days of mercantilism and colonialism). Meanwhile the wealthy nations continue to ensure that barriers exist against immigration and agriculture, so that "real" economic growth which results in a higher standard of living for the people has become more and more remote. Note that I use the term "real" economic growth to distinguish it from common economic indicators published by the World Bank, the International Monetary Fund, The World Trade Organization, and others. These indicators, using transfer figures, statistics from *maquiladoras*, and "exports" (which amount to one multinational in a poor country processing a segment of a product and then exporting it to a wealthy country for final completion), is hardly indicative of the true economic picture of a nation or of what free trade is meant to be.

The Pressure Valve

The Washington Consensus' one-size-fits-all, neoliberal globalization policy simply does not work for developing nations. Poor nations should be allowed to do what their rich neighbors did to become developed. They should not be forced to conform to the World Bank's *laissez-faire* approach. For a developing economy with low wages and low growth industries, this is the surest way to guarantee poverty. The result will be more illegal immigration, violence, and even terrorism as desperate populations take what options remain open to them. Most Washington analysts are well aware that one of the primary functions of immigration in the latter part of the 20th century has been to operate as a pressure valve for the ravaged economies of Central America and the Caribbean. Economies that had been crippled by natural disasters, by years of exploitation, by corporate greed, by U.S. intervention and manipulation, could tie up military resources for the next century; creating in Latin America a tumultuous bog of terror, war, and unrelenting hostility that would make the worst years of Viet Nam seem like a walk in the park.

To take but one glaring example in this century, the United States has had an active military presence in Central America for several decades. When you export a military force to another country, instead of a cultural and economic presence, the results are predictable.

The young people of El Salvador, for example, have learned a great deal from our years of intervention. However, they are not the things businessmen, scholars and teachers would have taught them. They are what young people learn from forces of occupation, from Yankee movies and young soldiers. Groups of teenagers there wear the colors of L.A. street gangs, graffiti abounds even on churches and cathedrals, and U.S. weapons make the slums of San Salvador one of the most dangerous places on the planet. Strong religious training, respect for elders, civic virtue, and a strong spiritual consciousness, values which characterize most Latin American countries, have been gradually eroded. How long before we've exported that culture of violence to other Latin American neighbors, where in combination with poverty and desperation it will pose a continuous threat to the security and sustainability of the Western Hemisphere?

Refugees

Each year millions of people are displaced by fratricidal wars, invasions by neighboring states, droughts, floods, earthquakes and famines. The number of refugees and asylum seekers world-wide in 2001 was 14,544,000. From ethnic cleansing in the Balkans and subsequent bombings by NATO warplanes fled hundreds of thousands. But not to the U.S., although the U.S. was instrumental in their displacement. They went to Germany, to Turkey, to Sweden, to

Belgium and Macedonia. Millions of people terrorized by the internecine warfare in the African states, by disease and famine, 3,346,000 to be exact, were forced from their homes. Again, they did not end up in the U.S.

People in the Congo fled to Cameroon, to Angola and the Central African Republic. People in Sierra Leone fled to Gambia, Guinea, Liberia and Nigeria. Refugees from Guatemala and El Salvador, Nicaragua and Colombia fled to Mexico, to Belize and Costa Rica. Refugees from the Palestine-Israeli conflict fled to Lebanon, Saudi Arabia, Yemen, and Syria. Much is made of how the United States is a haven for the politically oppressed, those displaced by terrorism, by famine, by war. In fact, the United States plays a very small role in the arena of refugee relief. Out of 14,444,000 refugees in 2001, the United States admitted 481,500. Less than Iran, less than Pakistan, less than Tanzania, and proportionally less than many smaller countries with far more limited resources. When one considers that in some instances the United States, by its military actions (the Balkans, Iraq and Afghanistan), by its undermining of popularly chosen governments (Guatemala, Nicaragua, El Salvador), and through its support of military regimes (Chile) and right wing paramilitary who kill civilians (Colombia) has been to a large extent responsible for several million of these displaced civilians, the claim that the United States is a benevolent and compassionate force on the world stage clearly is not supported by statistical data. In this era of globalization the United States has a glutton's share of the world market, the world's resources and the world's energy, but a miser's share of the world's responsibility for the alleviation of the misery, the disasters, the displacement, and the devastation that daily oppress its fellow global citizens (much of which it has directly or indirectly caused).

Reasons for an Immigration Policy

When we do allow immigrants into our country it is not because we are a nation of soft-hearted humanists. The number of refugees refused admittance to our country is clear evidence of that—whether it was Jews in the 1930s or Nicaraguans in the 1980s. Our national policy is opportunistic and self-referential. Although the United States is not averse to presenting the image of a nation committed to international altruism, national interest is always its primary motivation. So it is with immigration. There are practical reasons why we historically admitted immigrants, and without exception they were in our enlightened self-interest. They continue to be so. More productive people create more markets, and in a capitalist society growth is necessary for economic prosperity. Where are we going to export our cars and refrigerators? To Guatemala, where the average worker makes less than $2 a day? Unless we find ways of increasing capital investment, technology and growth in developing countries, stagnation and economic recession are inevitable without immigration.

The present U.S. birth rate indicates that couples are not even reproducing themselves in the 21st century. Without immigration there will be a net loss of labor for the productive and service markets, resulting in a lower standard of living for our children. Xenophobic and racial hysteria to the contrary, immigration adds to the strength of a nation. The more homogenous a people are, the weaker their line grows over time. Immigrants add a burst of energy to a nation and, while this often causes conflict, it serves to make a nation less decadent, less apathetic. Rome is a perfect example of what happens to a people who become isolationist and degenerate, while the million Irish added to the United States in the decade of 1840-1850 provides an example of how a nation is strengthened by an influx of immigrants who provide a new dynamic to a lethargic nation.

Demographics can change economic conditions, even if they do not immediately change attitudes. Italy, with Europe's lowest birthrate, will continue to need manpower. France's stock of unskilled labor is largely depleted. Nevertheless, xenophobia prevails in downtown Rome and Bologna, while in France the police wanted to pack thousands of illegal immigrants on trains until they were reminded that the French Jews were sent to "resettlement camps" by the Nazis in the 1940s. In

Pakistan, thousands of Hindus are forced to wear armbands identifying them as such—remnants of the shameful ghetto policy of the Hitler era.

Immigration Policy in the Future

The Bush-Fox immigration initiative failed in a divided Congress. An agreement to expand the guest-worker program and legalize currently employed illegal immigrants died in committee, although it had support from many sectors including the Catholic Church, and from many members of Congress including Republicans from the farm belt states. The guest-worker program would have dramatically reduced the number of illegal immigrants from Mexico—to about 150,000 last year—and saved the lives of migrants who died in the deserts and mountains of the Southwest. Legalization of currently employed illegals would simply regularize their status, and enable them to secure benefits to which their taxes and social security contributions have entitled them. It is now on President Obama's agenda but with even more divisive rhetoric likely to impede its progress. As the recession and U.S. unemployment take their toll, it seems unlikely that any statesmen (including the president) will risk political capital by carefully examining the economic benefits of immigration for the U.S. electorate.

Mexico, which incidentally has many thousands of people illegally entering its own boundaries each year, offers a "regularization program" to legalize documents (out-of-date tourist and student visas) and issue documents to those who have none. Many of these are retired U.S. and Canadian citizens who immediately become eligible for Mexican social security at a nominal fee; coverage which includes free hospitalization and reduced prescription costs. Something similar should be done in the U.S. A comprehensive agreement on border safety and guest-workers should include an equitable program in the United States for "regularization" of Mexicans.

The rich nations of the world, along with the World Bank and IMF, need to agree on a more pragmatic approach to developing nations. They should not be forced onto the fast track of globalization, privatization, free trade, and "comparative advantage" strategies. Insisting on the merits of the neoliberal system will result in rising poverty and increased levels of illegal immigration, as well as kidnapping and terrorism, as the more desperate poor take advantage of the only options available to them. The less developed nations should be allowed to do what the rich nations were allowed to do in order to get ahead. The United States could use its leadership in this area to force the IMF and World Bank to forego *laissez-faire* demands for low-wage, low-growth industries in Latin America.

The past twenty years have seen substantial liberalization throughout the world. Free-floating currencies, free flow of capital, lowering of trade barriers, and uneven but steady economic growth. During that same period, governments' control over the movement of people has tightened virtually everywhere. With the exception of the European Union, immigration controls are far tighter than they were a hundred years ago. As Bruce Scott notes, "the salient issue is that rich nations who laud liberalism and free markets are rejecting those very principles when they restrict freedom of movement."

We must move beyond "the one size fits all" economic blueprint for globalization, and see the inconsistencies in our ideologies. Then we need to develop a case by case model which will insure a healthy economy at home, as well as a secure and decent place for our neighbors in this hemisphere. This means a flexible immigration policy, divorced from rhetoric and self-serving moral justification on the one hand, and from isolationists, racist and xenophobic motivations on the other. Our immigration policy should serve the long-term interests of our hemisphere. It should be focused on economic development, flow of capital, and flow of workers in the Americas.

Europe, Africa and Asia are developing their own regional models, some faster, some slower. But our priority must be the security and sustainability of this hemisphere. For two centuries Mexico and the rest of Latin America have been low priorities except when it came to mercantile interests. Even today, once sees more in the newspapers and on television about Afghanistan, Iran, Palestine and Iraq. Not one of those nations poses the kind of danger to our national security that a turbulent, hungry, diseased, insolvent Latin America does. Not one of those nations promises so much in terms of long-term security, cultural diversity, and prosperity as does a Latin America which is secure, self-sufficient and productive.

NOTES

Immigration

"Will the Nation-State Survive Globalization?" by Martin Wolfe. *Foreign Affairs*. January/February 2001. pp. 178-190.

"The Great Divide in the Global Village." *Foreign Affairs*. January/February 2001. pp. 160-177.

"The Diversity Myth" by Benjamin Swartz. *The Atlantic Monthly*. May, 1995. pp. 57-69.

"Immigration: Is America Still A Melting Pot?" *Newsweek*. August 9, 1993. 6-15.

"Bush Aides Weigh Legalizing Status of Mexicans in U.S. *New York Times*. July 15, 2001.

Refugees

U.S. News & World Report. July 2, 2001, p. 9 "16,700 refugees received asylum in the U.S."

World Refugee Survey, 2001.
http://www.refugees.org/statistics/wrs01_table2.pdf

CHAPTER VII: THE GREEN REVOLUTION -
Mexican and Cuban Responses

The so-called Green Revolution was a managerial and technical export package from the U.S. to Latin America. It consisted of a complete plan to replace existing farming methods and crops with the more mechanized and scientific planting of high yield crops which were selected by geneticists for their response to chemical fertilizer and irrigation water, their resistance to pests, and in some cases their compatibility with mechanized harvesting and container shipping. It was touted as the answer to food shortages, a way to triple and even quadruple crop yields, and as a means to make Mexico self-sufficient for decades if not centuries to come, in feeding its growing population. The father of the Green Revolution in Mexico was an Iowa biologist by the name of Norman Borlaug.[1] He and his fellow scientists worked in a maize and wheat research center in Mexico which was funded by the Rockefeller Foundation and which ultimately produced new wheat strains which proved responsive to heavy doses of nitrogen and also highly resistant to pest and plant diseases. Borlaug, who had a street named after him in Hermosillo and received the Nobel Peace Prize in 1970 for his work, was almost universally hailed as a hero.

The first crop, widely planted in Mexico in the fifties and sixties, was a dwarf wheat called Norin 10. It was to be quickly followed by a hybrid maize. While these hybrids did increase crop yield significantly as promised, they brought other problems. They combined with mechanization to promote monoculture. Since single crops are more vulnerable than multiple crops to infestation, monoculture in turn brought the need for more and stronger pesticides, which poisoned water supplies and sickened agricultural workers.[2] Monoculture and the vast acreage it consumed gradually displaced subsistence farming, led to the gradual disappearance of other competing crops, and significantly reduced the varieties of wheat and corn available.

Since the Green Revolution favored large farmers who had both credit (for fertilizers and pesticides) and significant water resources for irrigation, small farmers gradually went bankrupt: their land was purchased cheaply from bank foreclosures and added to the already large holdings of the plutocracy. Biological diversity and plant resistance was lost, unemployed farm workers drifted to the cities creating acute social problems, and these frictions intensified into class and ethnic struggles such as the Chiapas uprising in 1994. Ironically, while before the Green Revolution Mexico was self-sufficient with regard to maize, by the mid-nineties it was importing a large percentage of corn from the U.S. to meet domestic needs. So, while there was an increase in crop yield per hectare, it did not bring prosperity, promote income distribution, result in agricultural independence or more and cheaper food for the Mexican people which was its alleged goal.

The Green Revolution not only radically transformed farming, it also fortified the unequal positions of wealth and power among a small group of landowners and government brokers, fundamentally affecting land and water quality, as well as the health and security of millions of people. It effectively destroyed the rural family, created political instability, and led to the overcrowding of Mexican cities along with chronic unemployment and poverty.

While token affirmation is generally given by most western governments to the principles of democracy, it should be noted that most of the actual economic decisions for the Green Revolution, such as importation of the new technology, introduction of hybrid crops, and the vast use of pesticides, all took place many steps removed from legitimate internal democratic decision-making on the part of the Mexican citizenry. The United States and Great Britain, hoping to influence the outcome of an upcoming election and get the Mexican government to reverse its position on the nationalization of oil companies, proposed the Rockefeller grant which funded the research center in Mexico. Subsequently, Ford Foundation funds for the starter crops were offered and readily accepted by Mexican officials.

Ironically, Mexico had no immediate need for this technology. At the time it was introduced, Mexico was fully able to feed its populace, there was no imminent famine in the land, pollution levels in the cities were lower than those of its northern neighbors, the rivers were clean, the air pure. Subsistence farming, while not creating any significant wealth, did in fact give millions a living, provided a healthy and peaceful countryside, and supported strong families while ensuring minimal unemployment and low immigration. The desire of British and U.S. firms for petroleum revenue and access to Mexican oil fields led to the hard sell and "free" offers of technological and scientific support to Mexico for this project. But beware Greeks bearing gifts, as Homer noted 4,000 years ago. And as Chomsky reminded us more recently, "The nature of the American state is to maximize global control in the interests of the dominant domestic groups. If someone doesn't accept these assumptions, he can't be part of the system."[3]

By the 1990s, as a direct result of these innovations, 40% of Mexicans were living below the subsistence level, with less to eat than the minimal daily U.N. requirement. Poverty had increased 25% from the pre-Green Revolution, pre-NAFTA period; unemployment and inner-city crime were rampant. Homelessness which rarely existed two decades before was now commonplace, as more and more people were displaced from the countryside.

The air was so polluted with poisons and particulates that school children often could not play outside in the winter months in Mexico City; more than a third of the grain consumed by the populace was imported; the water table was essentially desiccated through irrigation of monoculture crops for export, and the Mexican family was decimated by rural exodus to cities to find jobs or by immigration to the U.S. Meanwhile, Mexico had one of the largest economic "growth rates" in Latin America, the largest number of billionaires per capita, and was a favorite of foreign investors.

In Cuba, on the other hand, something quite different happened. Cuba's history of a sugar monoculture, accentuated by mechanization with Russian machinery from the early sixties through the eighties which kept the island economically afloat, came to an abrupt halt with the collapse of the USSR and the advent of a relentless U.S. economic embargo. Without oil to run their tractors, without pesticides and fertilizers, with little electric power and no public transportation, the world waited for the collapse of the Cuban economy. It was expected that before the people literally starved to death, they would overthrow Castro, and that the U.S. would rescue the island from famine and mismanagement. At first, things happened as U.S. planners predicted. With no market for the sugar, no funds to purchase imported food, the caloric intake on the island dropped from 3,000 calories per day to 1,900 according to U.N. statistics.[4]

But Castro had other ideas. He stopped exporting sugar, reversed the monoculture agricultural policy, turned agricultural collectives into small private farms, and encouraged the planting of thousands of urban gardens. Since the Cubans had little in the way of fertilizers or pesticides, they turned to organic gardening, using compost and worms to aerate and fertilize the soil, natural plants and natural seeds, as well as a combination of man-made and natural pest control (such as utilizing selected strains of bacteria and raising beneficial insects). The government, realizing that the efficiency of this kind of program would be highly dependent on the technical know-how of its citizens, invested heavily in secondary and university education, ensuring that reliable chemical, agricultural and biological expertise would be available to the citizenry. Not only did the caloric intake quickly return to previous levels and beyond, but the small farmers began making a profit, the air was cleaner, the soil was richer, the water purer, and the citizens healthier. Even in the capital city, Havana, the planned used of space and organic farming yielded 300,000 tons of food which was nearly the total vegetable supply for the entire city.[5] Tens of thousands of city people today are employed in this agribusiness and most make a sustainable wage.

I am aware of the argument that Cuba is a dictatorial regime, that the centralist planning which sponsored this system is inherently flawed and deprives the citizens of their human rights. However, let's compare the system with that of Mexico. There, too, the system was imposed on the people without any vote or decision-making on their part. There, too, the decision was a central one, affecting the rights and freedoms of individual farmers and workers. However, the differences are considerable. In the so-called "democratic" system of Mexico, the workers were displaced; the farmers lost their land, agribusiness created an enormous export market as well as a dozen billionaires, while the people slowly starved to death. Today the cities grow more polluted, the land is salinized from irrigation residue, the rivers are choked with chemicals, and the country itself is dependent on external supplies of grain.

Whereas in Cuba, thanks to Castro's foresight, the citizenry is fully employed, well fed, the air is pollution free, the land is fertile and free of chemicals, and—despite the Marxist label—hundreds of thousands make a profit off the surplus produce that they sell.

William James once warned about the prejudice that passes for thinking when we look at any set of facts from the perspective of an ideology. What we should see when we look at Castro's experiment is simply what is useful, how it works, and how might we be able to incorporate elements of it. This is the pragmatic approach to solving problems and the one that makes the most sense. As a pragmatist, I frankly don't care about Edison's politics, or Bill Gates' economic theories. I want to know if the electricity works and if my computer program will run. Yet, so much foreign and domestic policy, affecting the daily lives of millions of innocent souls, is crafted by ideologues who rarely venture beyond academia or Capitol Hill or Los Pinos. They are like the farmer in Robert Frost's poem who cannot get past his father's saying ("Good fences make good neighbors") and likes it so well that he repeats it over and over without regard for whether it has any real relevance to the reality of New England farming.

Obviously, the complete solution to the problem of world hunger is not on Castro's island. But neither is the answer to a sustainable living environment to be found in the agribusiness plants of Iowa, abandoned farms and rural towns of Nebraska; poisoned rivers, choked towns and highways from Texas to Mexico City. There is not one answer but many. And there is likely no single global land-use system that is workable, but a multiplicity of complex and local solutions available to different societies, operating under different geographical and climatic conditions, subject to different cultural and societal influences, with varied gifts and needs.

We must first recognize the fraud that is perpetrated by corporate and governmental globalists who, while comfortably dealing with state terrorists from Saudi Arabia and Israel, reject the successful policies of Cuban agronomists, the equally successful experiments of Venezuelan economists, and the peaceful protests of Mexican farmers at Cancún. The question we should ask ourselves is this: What combination of policies would lead to a better quality of life for the citizens of the individual countries, instead of power accumulating in the hands of multi-national corporations, degradation of the environment, denigration of the citizenry, and the waging of incessant war financed by the largest military state on the planet? No single ideology can answer this question, for the simple reason that ideology is driven by an abstract agenda—not by the dynamic realities of people's actual lives, the lands where they grow their food, the air they breathe and the water they drink. As Wendell Berry wrote so eloquently:

> The answers, if they are to come and if they are to work, must be developed in the presence of the user and the land....Good agriculture and good forestry cannot be invented by self-styled smart people in the offices and laboratories of a centralized economy and then sold at the highest possible profit to supposedly dumb country people....And it does not matter how the methodologies are labeled; whether 'industrial,' or 'conventional,' 'organic,' or 'sustainable,' the professional or professorial condescension that is blind to the primacy of the union between individual people and individual places is ruinous.[6]

NOTES:

1. *Something New Under the Sun* by J.R. McNeill. W.W. Norton & Co. New York, 2000, pp. 221-222.

2. *Ibid.*, p. 221, n. 66.

3. *Latin American: From Colonization to Globalization* by Noam Chomsky. Ocean Press. Melbourne, 1999.

4. "The Cuba Diet" by Bill McKibben. *Harpers*. April 2005, pp. 61-69.

5. *Ibid.,* p. 63.

6. *What Are People For?* by Wendell Berry. North Point Press. New York, 1998, pp. 114-115.

CHAPTER VIII: BIRTH CONTROL - WHO GETS THE RIGHT TO CHOOSE?

Ever since *Roe versus Wade*, the United States has legitimized and politicized abortion. It is a domestic decision that seems to have the approval of the majority of the electorate, although there remains a vociferous minority who, whether through religious principles or logic, find the "right to choose" incompatible with the right to life guaranteed by the constitution. It is not my intention to present a brief for either side. However, a foreign policy which exports sterilization techniques, contraception and abortion implements, and a World Bank policy (supported by the U.S.) which makes credit dependent upon a birth control program, violate both the internal sovereignty of the nations so compromised, and the much vaulted "freedom to choose" which is the hallmark of the U.S. domestic agenda.

Family planning has been shown to increase as the educational level of the country increases. Family planning in Latin America and elsewhere, however, may or may not mean limitation of the size of the family. There may be some instances when it makes perfect sense to have a large family. Would Rose Kennedy have wished to have one less child? Would a mother in Colombia who lost four of her sons to army massacres? Would the Jewish parents living on the Gaza strip or the Canadian farmer cutting hay on his family acres?

Various U.S. missionary groups have gone to Brazil's Amazonian territory and sterilized thousands of indigenous women living there. Amazonia is one of the least inhabited, least dense of all the areas in the world. Whose interests are being served here? The practice will merely hasten the inevitable demise of the indigenous people in this part of the world, thus facilitating the takeover of their lands by multinationals. Sterilization is cheaper and less bloody than machine guns, and less likely to cause a stir in the international press. But the result is the same. It is the 21st century's answer to the genocide which was practiced against indigenous people in a much more violent way on the Great Plains of North America.

The United States, along with the World Bank and family planning foundations, are the new emissaries for population control in developing countries. The image of these entities in the world press appears less harsh than that of China, for example, which provides jail terms and mutilation for parents who dare to have more than one child. However, in actual fact, the result is the same. Moreover, at least in China the decisions are made by Chinese for the perceived benefit of the Chinese people. In Latin America the decisions are made by the World Bank and by U.S. policy makers, financiers, and foundations whose real interest is not the welfare of the individual countries but rather their own profits and security.

Most Latin American countries do not, in fact, have a surplus of people. A trip through the countryside of Mexico, Brazil, Chile, Ecuador, or Guatemala would convince even the most skeptical U.S. citizen of that. Hundreds of kilometers of territory have no inhabitants at all. Millions of hectares of land lie fallow and unproductive because there is no capital available to irrigate them. Millions more are devoted to the production of grains, produce and cattle for export while the people starve. The situation in Latin America is reminiscent of the Great Hunger in Ireland in the 1840s where Great Britain exported thousands of tons of grain from the country while half the people were systematically starved to death. Birth control was suggested then as the solution to Ireland's crisis, but the Irish were considered too much in the thrall of Papism to ever see it as a benefit. It might be argued, however, that when one's race is being exterminated, birth control might simply appear as another device of the exterminator, regardless of economic benefits.

In a well-known work by Jonathan Swift called "A Modest Proposal" it was even suggested that, since the Irish Catholics would continue to produce babies, that the babies be butchered and exported as meat ("tender as suckling pig") for the British market. This would provide income for Irish parents while at the same time solving the balance of payments problem for the island nation. Although intended as a satire, many readers took it seriously.

Eduardo Galeano in his book *Open Veins of Latin America* notes that the some wag wrote on a wall in La Paz, Bolivia, "Help fight poverty. Kill a beggar." This graffiti humor is reminiscent of Swift but just as subject to misunderstanding. Many philanthropic and missionary organizations have been doing just that: killing beggars, but killing them in the womb before they have an opportunity to beg, steal, fight for justice, or simply be part of the new millennium. We should be ashamed.

But, of course, we're not. We see thousands of immigrants coming into California, New Mexico and Arizona and think that birth control is an obvious and humanistic solution. Our perception that this problem could be simply solved with universal birth control is a result of what we are not being told by our press and by our government. We are not told, for example, that El Salvador, Nicaragua and Honduras have lower population densities than England. That Brazil and Chile have seventeen times fewer people per square mile than Japan. That Mexico has a lower population density than Ireland. In most Latin American countries the problem is not that there are too many people. The crises that cause immigration to the north are similar in kind to those which caused the flight of the Irish from the British Isles, and left that nation poor, backward and empty of people for the next hundred years.

In 1992, the *Roe versus Wade* decision was revisited by the Supreme Court, and this time the justices noted the importance of both the waiting period and the parental permission element suggested by the State of Pennsylvania. The language of their decision is critical because it makes a statement about individual liberties which many North Americans have advocated for themselves while denying them to others.

> The mother who carries a child to full term is subject to anxieties, to physical constraints, to pain that only she must bear. That these sacrifices have from the beginning of the human race been endured by woman with a pride that ennobles her in the eyes of others and gives to the infant a bond of love cannot alone be grounds for the State to insist that she make the sacrifice. Her suffering is too intimate and personal for the State to insist, without more, upon its own vision of the woman's role, however dominant that role may be in the course of our history and our culture. The destiny of woman must be shaped to a large extent by her own concept of her spiritual imperatives and her place in society.[1]

Abortion is an intimate and personal matter, according to our Supreme Court justices, which should be decided by the mother and her "own conceptions of her spiritual imperatives and her place in society." Are we willing to concede that the indigenous woman in Amazonia has the same right as the housewife in New Jersey? Will we grant that the beliefs of a Catholic in Colombia should be accorded the same respect as those of a Methodist in Connecticut? If not, then we should re-read *Animal Farm*, George Orwell's fable about totalitarianism wherein the central rule that once governed the society ("All animals are created equal") was changed ("Some are more equal than others").

The United States has decided for its own nation that the right of a woman to choose is fundamental. It has also decided that the State has the right to take the lives of certain criminal offenders. Mexico, along with most other developed nations, has done away with capital punishment considering it barbaric and unworthy of a democratic republic. Mexico also, while encouraging women's education and family planning, has continued to support the right to life as a national policy. It does not export its doctrines via missionaries to its neighbors. Neither should the United States export theirs. Nor should the United States use its political and economic muscle in world organizations to provide birth control as a solution to economic policies which have impoverished these populations.

This seems clear to me and to my Mexican students as well. The question my students then raise is: Why does the U.S. continue to do so? I'm obliged to bite my tongue because the answers which seem most apparent are (a) U.S. citizens' perception of their neighbors to the South as inferior (*They don't know any better and will continue making babies until they starve themselves to death*); (b) the belief that Catholic religion is taken too seriously in Latin America, and to the detriment of the people (*What the Pope tells them, they do);* (c) the belief that these are macho cultures run by ignorant and aggressive men where women are not allowed to choose for themselves; and (d) the presumption that the United States' economic dominance also reflects its moral, cultural, intellectual and social superiority over Latin America. Is this not a correct assessment? Is this not the real truth which I am embarrassed to share with my students? This is what I perceive when I return home on my New England visits after working in Latin America. Greeting me at the customs booth last year was a young INS agent, who asked where I had been. I told him that I had been living and working as a teacher in Mexico for the past two decades. He looked at me like I was bit touched then asked, "Why on earth would you want to live there?"

The questions and preconceptions noted above are all part of an economic imperialism which is difficult to expunge. U.S. citizens have been taught to believe that their 200 years of history are somehow more sacred than Mexico's two thousand; that Mexico's rich and ancient culture ("Colonial" in Mexico means the 1500s, not the 1700s as in the States) is somehow less than that of their northern neighbor's; that the Day of the Dead is barbaric while Halloween is delightful, and that if anybody were more cultured or smarter than North Americans they'd be just as rich and powerful. Mexico and most Latin American countries (so the argument goes) are not rich or powerful, hence they are backward, undeveloped and regressive. Their history and culture can be ignored even by U.S. citizens who claim to be educated. This attitude combines economic imperialism with cultural barbarism, exploiting Latin American nations on the one hand while denying their history, their values, their culture and their imperatives for existence on the other.

It is strange to me that even thinkers who are in most other respects aware of the economic disasters perpetrated by multinationals, and the economic crises perpetrated so that the U.S. might have favorable trade agreements, nevertheless propose the decimation of Latin American people as a solution. It is a simplistic, selfish and narrow world view. To most educated Latin Americans it appears to be *lo real mágico* or a U.S. version of surrealism. In the words of Eduardo Galeano:

> Those who deny liberation to Latin America also deny our only possible rebirth, and incidentally absolve the existing structures for blame. Our youth multiplies, rises, listens: what does the voice of the system offer? The system speaks a surrealist language. In lands that are empty it proposes to avoid births, in countries where capital is plentiful but wasted it suggests that capital is lacking; it describes as "aid" the deforming orthopedics of loans and the draining of wealth that results from foreign investment; it calls upon big landowners to carry out agrarian reforms and upon the oligarchy to practice social justice. The class struggle only exists, we are told, because foreign agents stir it up; but social classes do exist and the oppression of one by the other is known as the Western way of life.[2]

Lest there still be a doubt in the reader's mind about the motivations behind the birth control, abortion and sterilization programs instituted in Latin America, let's look at the population densities of the countries involved, and compare them to some of their "developed" counterparts.

Mexico has 127 inhabitants per square mile, while Israel has 688. I haven't heard anyone suggesting the sterilization of Jewish mothers lately. Yet, Israel's population density is 5.4 times that of Mexico and spilling over into areas previously inhabited by indigenous Arab communities. Could it be there are political, perhaps even racist overtones to the birth control agenda in Latin America?

Let's not jump to conclusions. Perhaps a comparison with European figures would be fairer. Colombia has 84 inhabitants per square mile, Germany has 606. Brazil 49, Great Britain 621. Argentina 32, Luxembourg 416. Venezuela 62, Italy 492. Hmm. These results seem to be even more damning than the Israel comparison.[3]

Mexico (127) has about the same population density as Ireland (131) and most South and Central American countries have even fewer inhabitants.[4] While population control is a priority in countries such as India, Pakistan, China and parts of Africa, it is not and has never been a creditable solution to Latin America's problems. What Latin America needs is the freedom to develop independently of external controls on its economy, to be free of outside interference in its political development, to be respected for its culture and history, and to be allowed to address its social problems with innovative and responsible solutions without them being labeled "communistic" when they put foreign capital at risk, and to establish protections for local industry without being penalized by the World Bank or the IMF. Given a chance to do these things, national industries will continue to develop, the growing population will lead to an increase in production and consumption, savings will grow, and thus internal investment will increase. The so-called "undeveloped" countries of Latin America will create economic growth at their own pace, providing internal safeguards for their industries and their workers, protecting their environments, and strengthening their national cultures and identities. If they are truly our neighbors, why would be wish them any less?

The problem is not birth control but rather demographics, which is to say, distribution of population. Most of the problems resulting from urban population densities have been caused by globalization, free transfer of investment capital and industry without concomitant investment in, or concern for, labor. In fact, the "flexibility of the labor force" (a favorite neoliberal phrase), simply means keeping labor insecure and dependent, undermining unions, controlling wages, and shifting production locales when one labor force begins to prosper, to another site where labor can be obtained more cheaply. The manipulation of labor by multinationals, and the avoidance of tax obligations, has resulted in more people living in congested areas coupled with a lack of social services or urban infrastructure to insure a decent quality of life.

Loss of population has so impinged upon the fabric of some countries that it is entirely possible their nationhood will disappear as a viable economic and cultural entity. In Uruguay, for example, the country's birth rate for 2002 exceeded its death rate by only 20,000 and the population continues to grow older. While in the United States this trend is offset by immigration, the opposite trend is occurring in Uruguay. Already one of the least-populated countries in South America, Uruguay has lost over 54,000 inhabitants over the past year and a half to immigration. Gradually the country is being marginalized and falling behind its economic partners in Mercosur: Argentina, Brazil and Paraguay.[5] According to a report from the North American Congress on Latin America (NACLA), if current birth rates continue, by the year 2050 Uruguay will constitute less than 1.3% of Mercosur and will be well on its way to extinction as a viable economic entity.[6] As social services become more imperiled by the lack of a tax base, as economic opportunities disappear for lack of employable youth, those who remain are more and more marginalized and inclined to move out as well. Polls by the firm Equpos/Mori show that 22% of Uruguayans are considering moving abroad. What happens to culture, to family, to history, tradition, folklore and sense of identity when a country is only a geographical spot on the map with no people to fill its churches, its libraries, its museums? No children to sing its songs, no poets to write its stories, no one to farm its land or build its bridges? In the 21st century will it be as strange to find someone from Uruguay as someone from Camelot?

There are several sacred cows in the history of economic and social development. The unassailable value of birth control is one of the least examined. Hidden under the rubric of "family planning" (couldn't you plan to have <u>more</u> children?) birth control is a classic example of what Milan Kundera called the "obstinate persistence of unexamined ideas." It is time to take a look at it again in the light of new evidence and to suggest that, as is the case with so many dichotomies, there may be a third approach which is more humane, more logical and more appropriate for Latin America.

NOTES

1. *Planned Parenthood v. Casey*, 505 U.S. 833 (1992).

2. Eduardo Galeano, *Upside Down*. Metropolitan Books. New York, 2000.

3. Population density figures are obtained by dividing the latest census figures for the population for the given country by the number of square miles in that nation. Sources which formed the basis for these calculations included the *U.N. Demographic Yearbook*, the U.S. *Census Bureau International Database* and the *2003 World Almanac*. St. Martin Press. New York, 2003.

4. Op.cit.

5. Andrés Guadín, "Uruguay: Population Trends Impede Development." *NACLA: Report on the Americas.* Vol. XXXVII No. 3. Nov/Dec 2003, pp. 46-47.

6. *Ibid.,* p. 67

CHAPTER IX: SAVAGE SUBSIDIES

Few U.S. citizens are aware of the incredible resentment caused by the policy of subsidizing agricultural products which are dumped on the international market, while insisting that manufactured goods, in which the U.S. has a competitive advantage, be strictly subject to the laws of free trade.

It is estimated that governments of developed countries, largely the United States and the European Union, provide more than $300 million[1] in domestic support and export subsidies for agricultural products: most notably sugar, cotton and corn which depress world market prices, diminish the earnings of poor countries and prevent them from competing with the developed world's artificially low prices. This is one of the major reasons that, despite the proclaimed economic advantages of "free trade" and the Washington Consensus[2], the poverty in Latin America has doubled over the past decade.

The economic competitive advantage of countries such as Brazil and Guatemala is that they can grow and harvest sugar cheaper than the United States. Mexico can produce corn cheaper and Argentina, beef. However, subsidies to agricultural conglomerates in the developed countries have created an artificially lower price whose net result is an economic depression in these Latin American countries, abandonment of farm and ranch lands, and—in Mexico—the net importation of corn from the United States. Mexico at least has some leverage to fight back since it is the United States' largest trading partner. Recently it has sought an exemption from the Canadian and U.S. agreement to eliminate tariffs from all agricultural imports. Mexico has been negotiating a side agreement which will exempt beans and white corn from the tariff elimination process. Regardless of the outcome, opposition leaders in the Mexican Congress will make the agricultural aspects of NAFTA a major issue in the coming years.[3]

The West and Central African nations (Chad, Mali, Benin and Burkina Faso) produce cotton five times cheaper than the United States and it accounts for 80% of their exports. However, with 4 billion[4] in subsidies to its own cotton farmers, the United States is able to flood the market with "cheaper" cotton, thus simultaneously bleeding the U.S. taxpayer and poor Africans. Nor do the subsidies protect independent U.S. farmers, since they go mostly to massive agribusiness corporations. Subsidies are, in effect, corporate welfare provided by successive administrations that have removed safety nets for marginal workers, cut food stamps and welfare, while transferring the surplus thus provided to double-dipping corporate agribusinesses. When a representative group of African nations at the Cancún Conference called for an immediate elimination of subsidies on cotton because they were destroying the livelihoods of African farmers and impeding development in the region, their proposal was greeted with contempt by the U.S. delegation. One U.S. negotiator reportedly quipped, "Create a larger demand for T-shirts!"[5] The depths of resentment and even hatred that encounters such as these create abroad are considerable, and undermine the United States' legitimacy as a world leader. According to the *New York Times*:

> Any hope that the United States would take a moral high
> ground at Cancún, and reclaim its historic leadership in pressing
> for freer trade, was further dashed by the disgraceful manner in
> which U.S. negotiators rebuffed the rightful demands of West
> African nations that the United States commit itself to a clear
> phasing out of its harmful cotton subsidies. U.S. business and
> labor groups, not to mention taxpayers, should be enraged that
> the administration seems more solicitous of protecting the most
> indefensible segment of United States protectionism rather than
> protecting the national interest by promoting economic growth
> through trade.[6]

A report by the Carnegie Endowment, an independent Washington research group, found that after ten years of NAFTA, Mexico was worse off than it was before it signed the agreement. Jobs in the manufacturing service sectors had fallen by 2%. But those who suffered the worst were the farmers "who were adversely affected by falling prices for their crops, especially corn,"[7] a problem intensified by the lowered tariff barriers to U.S.-grown corn which because of farm subsidies could be sold at a lower price than the domestic Mexican commodity.

This issue of subsidies is interesting, too, in the light of the U.S. public's negative attitude toward foreign aid (less than 1% of the federal budget). We give more economic aid to multinational corporations to increase their profits than we do to all the countries in the world combined. And if we were to end those subsidies tomorrow, as the African delegation suggested at Cancún, the economic growth of those countries exporting their products at market prices would obviate the necessity for more foreign aid. Another boon to the U.S. taxpayer.

In Miami two months after the Cancún walkout, there was a conference to formulate guidelines for the new Free Trade Area of the Americas (FTAA), a plan by the Bush administration to construct a set of rules upon which economic relations in the Western Hemisphere would be organized. Knowing the inconsistencies, inequalities and disruption that NAFTA caused in Mexico, Miami became a site for protests by union leaders, environmentalists, feminists and workers' groups. Their suppression by the Miami police was both brutal and unprecedented. According to a report filed by Rebecca Solnit there were over 200 demonstrators arrested and over 100 injured, most as a result of tear gas, pepper spray and blows to the head and face by police batons. People were pulled from their cars at gunpoint outside the International Hotel in Miami: "mostly white, mostly labor organizers, environmentalists and religious…"[8] who saw the dangers inherent in another NAFTA-like agreement which would despoil the lands of Central America, pollute its rivers, dislocate its farmers and plunge the economies into a nose dive similar to that experienced by Mexico after the signing of the 1994 accord.

Ms. Solnit's comparison of the two agreements is not accidental. FTAA is an agreement which the current administration touts as having many of the same "benefits" as NAFTA. However, a close look at the results of the agreement over the past ten years show that besides loss of growth in the Mexican sector and the displacement of farmers, "close to 400,000 jobs have been lost in the U.S. since NAFTA with new jobs paying, on average, only 77 percent of the wages of their earlier employment."[9] So that explains why the labor leaders and union members were there in Miami—ten thousand of them.

The FTAA, as presently written, could force countries throughout Central America to accept genetically modified foods. "Being forced to buy expensive patented seeds every season, rather than saving and planting their own, will force traditional subsistence farmers in the developing world into dependency on transnational corporations and closer to the brink of starvation."[10] Of course, that's the point. But, lest we think this is a Central or South American problem, keep in mind that more than 80% of the planet's biodiversity in corn and potatoes is in Latin America. If that biodiversity disappears and a virus infects the common Idaho potato which is now the one most commonly grown and sold today, the result will make the Irish Famine look like a walk in the park, not to mention what will happen to lovers of McDonald's french fries, deprived of their staple until the end of time.

As to the environmentalists, they know that since NAFTA "fifteen wood product companies from the U.S. have set up operations in Mexico, and logging there has increased dramatically. In the Mexican state of Guerrero, 40 percent of the forests have been lost in the last eight years, and massive clear-cutting has led to soil erosion and habitat destruction."[11] Those who risked being assaulted and imprisoned in Miami to protest the destruction of the U.S. middle class, the right to fair wages, the preservation of a strong labor force and the conservation of the last remaining oxygen sources in our hemisphere were doing work which honored us all. The contempt with which they were treated is akin to the contempt with which Martin Luther King was treated when he was similarly beaten and imprisoned in the U.S. South after he spoke up to protect the right and dignity of human beings fifty years ago.

The U.S proposal of the FTAA is not a method for shaping a global accord. It is rather a plan for a regional agreement in which U.S.-based multinationals have an economic advantage and are provided with preferential positions. So, while the administration preaches free trade and globalization, what it is actually seeking is a restriction on globalization with a competitive advantage for multinationals based in the United States rather than those based in the Far East or Europe.

This in itself would not be wholly objectionable as it would simply encourage competition between regions. However, there is little that is "free" in it, either as free trade or as *laissez-faire* non-government interference in the market. It is direct manipulation of the market and so we have a gap both in ideology and in credibility.

U.S. labor unions and even the National Association of Manufacturers in the U.S. have suggested that the FTAA should not be approved by Congress unless there are revisions in the agreement for labor and environmental accords.[12] The U.S. Chamber of Commerce, most multinationals, and the Bush administration on the other hand were "flexible" on these issues because, of course, low wages and lack of environmental accords are exactly what allow large companies to make disproportionate profits. The price though, is high: child labor, brutal conditions, lack of social services, destruction of lakes and rivers, deforestation—and not one the businesses will have to pay. These costs will be absorbed by the host countries in terms of loss of potable drinking water, disease, fetus malformation, polluted air and generations of physically and mentally marginalized citizens. They will also be absorbed by the U.S. taxpayer in terms of increased unemployment, global warming, increased immigration, anti-U.S sentiment, and a less secure world. Add to this the displacement of hundreds of thousands of farmers who can no longer make a living on the land due to agricultural subsidies and the flooding of the market with the products of those subsidies, and you have a cauldron of civic unrest, domestic disorder, and the violence born of desperation throughout Latin America.

When Henry Ford opened his factory in Dearborn, Michigan he had a revolutionary new theory. His idea was to mass produce automobiles, pay his workers a fair wage, and sell the automobile at a price his workers could afford. The idea worked, resulting in generations of highly paid workers, market growth, new designs and technological advances, and increased prosperity for his nation. He did not find the cheapest materials, the lowest paid workers; he did not move his plant to Guatemala or Cambodia. The reason: he wanted to create a larger market for his cars, not just sell them to the affluent. Ford knew that if he wanted his business to continue to grow, and the economy to grow, he needed to create customers for his products. In the process he provided business to the steel mills, the tire factories, to oil speculators and refineries. He provided millions of jobs to upholsterers, mechanics, oil workers, traffic cops and construction workers. And he sold more cars.

This sane economic reasoning has been lost on the new generation of global marketers. They want to move the companies to areas where the labor force is most mobile, most desperate and cheapest, and where the environmental laws are most lax. We are already seeing the inevitable results. The increase in inventory of hard manufactured goods, growing poverty in Latin America, irreparable damage to the environment, loss of employment in the United States, and recession.

A factory worker in Mexico making $300 a month cannot purchase a new Ford. An electronics assembler in Guatemala making $45 a week cannot afford the digital camera or computer she assembles. If the workers in the factories where the products are produced cannot afford to buy those products, what is the result? Short-term profits for a few manufacturers, cheaper prices for a few buyers, but—ultimately—stagnation, lack of growth, because even though more units are being produced, there are fewer people with the wages or savings to purchase them.

When United States Trade Representative Robert B. Zoellick stated that opponents of globalization might have had "intellectual connections"[13] with terrorists he was signaling a very dangerous formulation which is part of the Newspeak which underlies an ideological divide as far from Henry Ford's model of capitalism as the World Bank is from Jeffersonian democracy. What the new formulation consists of is a combination of cooperate greed and anti-populist ideology which seeks to derive short-term economic advantage from the marketplace while destroying the economy now for the poor, ten years from now for the middle class, and a generation from now for those who will inherit the no-growth companies and paper wealth their forebears accumulated.

There are, of course, alternatives. They don't appear on CNN or in White House press releases. However, they do exist. The policies that now encompass globalization are, in fact, merely corporate strategies marketed as global priorities and supported by those few who have their fingers in this very rich pie. It is in their self-interest to convince the public that there are no real alternatives, that free trade equals democracy, that its opponents are either communists promoting class conflict or intellectual bunkmates of international terrorists. In fact, there are hundreds of thousands around the world who are creating grassroots alternatives to this corporate globalization. Citizen groups composed of workers, small business people, investment counselors, doctors, attorneys, economists, teachers and scientists from around the world who have formulated the "Alternative Agreement for the Americas"[14] which offers a view of what a totally responsible and environmentally sustainable economy in this hemisphere would look like. You can find this document on the Global Exchange website. [15]

The media tells us largely by its silence, that there is little happening in Latin America besides earthquakes, hungry masses and economic chaos. When proposals such as NAFTA and FTAA are decided on, when international economic conferences in Cancún or Miami are reported on, the media tells us that the protests outside the conferences are organized by anarchists and radicals whom the police need to keep in check to maintain public order. We are told that we are blessed to be living in the United States and that the problems of the

Third World are ones we should let the experts in trade, finance and diplomacy take care of. Never in the course of human history has that been less true, never has the U.S. citizen's knowledge and awareness been more important. We need to be proactive; we need to ask questions of our representatives in Congress, read alternative versions of events on ZNet, Alterinfos, and other alternative publications[16] and sites which report economic and social news of the hemisphere that affects us daily.

As Noam Chomsky once wrote in another time and place:

Whether they're called "liberal" or "conservative", the major media are large corporations, owned by and interlinked by larger conglomerates. Like other corporations they sell a product to the market. The market is advertisers, that is, other businesses. The product is audiences…There are systems of illegitimate authority in every corner of the social, political, economic and cultural worlds. For the first time in human history, we have to face the problem of protecting an environment that can sustain a decent human existence. We don't know that honest and dedicated effort will be enough to resolve or mitigate such problems as these. We can be quite confident that the lack of such efforts will spell disaster.[17]

Notes

1. John Ross, quoted in "Stop Racing to the Bottom." *The Progressive*, November, 2003, p. 8.

2. The term "Washington Consensus" is now synonymous with market fundamentalism applied globally. It was first used by economist John Williamson in 1989 to describe the agreement between the World Bank, the International Monetary Fund and he U.S. Treasury Department on those policies which would best promote economic reform in Latin America while, at the same time, promoting U.S. interests.

3. *NACLA: Report on the Americas*. Vol. XXXVII, May/June, 2003, p.5.

4. Teo Ballvé, "Globalization Resistance in Cancún." *NACLA: Report on the Americas.* Vol. XXXVIII, Nov./Dec., 2003, p.17.

5. *Ibid.,*p. 10.

6. "Harvesting poverty: The Cancún Failure," *New York Times* (on-line headline service), September 16, 2003.

7. *NACLA: Report on the Americas*. Vol. XXXVII, May/June, 2003, p.5.

8. Celia W. Dugger, "Report Finds Few Benefits for Mexico in NAFTA." *New York Times* (on-line headline service). November 19, 2003.

9. Rebecca Solnit. "Report from Miami." <Tomdispatch.com> November 25, 2003.

10. "Ten Reasons to Oppose the FTAA." *Global Exchange*. December, 2003, p. 1.

11. "Stop Racing to the Bottom." *The Progressive*, p. 9

12. *Global Exchange, op. cit.* p.2.

13. "House Leaders Urge Halt to Business, Labor, Environmental Effort." *Inside U.S. Trade*, February 16, 2001.

14. Quoted by William Finnegan in "The Economics of Empire" from *Harpers Magazine*, May, 2003, p. 41.

15. Available at www.zmag.org simply check the index.

16. www.zmag.org; www.alterinfos.org; see also www.orionline.org. MIT professor Noam Chomsky contributes many articles to the ZMagazine site and with his volunteer research staff and friends around the world provides an alternative view of the economy and of social and political conditions. Wendell Berry is a frequent contributor to the Orion site who offers alternatives to the corporate view of a globalized economy. Another important alternative resource is www.america.org. which is the Center for America's Connection to the Americas.

17. Noam Chomsky, *What Uncle Sam Really Wants*. Odonian Press. Tucson, 1992, pp. 93-100.

CHAPTER X: LOST LIVES AND IMPOVERISHED SOULS - The Failure of the Church in Latin America

When the conservative Catholic cardinal Joseph Ratzinger was elected Pope Benedict XVI, many observers saw this as the beginning of a reactionary period for the Catholic Church; with the Cardinal's well-known opposition to female clergy, gay unions, cloning, freedom of choice, ecumenical movements, use of contraceptives to prevent AIDS, liberation theology, community organization of lay Catholics, and social activism. To those who have followed the politics of the Church in Latin America, however, his election came as no surprise and is clearly seen, not as a new position of the Church, but one which began in the 1980s.

Cardinal Ratzinger, well-known as the Vatican enforcer for Pope John Paul, ordered the 1984 "silencing" of liberation theologians, forbidding them to publish their work, and removing bishops who supported their views; as well as declaring Rome's opposition to the social activism and organizations for self-help which priests in impoverished regions had long regarded as central to their Christian mission.

To understand what this has meant to poor and disenfranchised populations in Latin America and what the election of this cardinal to the papacy is likely to mean in the years ahead, it is useful to look back at recent history—most notably in Central America.

El Salvador: Archbishop Oscar Romero was a traditional prelate when appointed to his position in El Salvador in the 70s. What made him exceptional as time passed was that he paid attention to the poor and disenfranchised in his congregation. He listened when they told him stories of family members kidnapped by government death squads, when they tried to organize agricultural workers, or when they spoke out against government policies of repression. He looked at the pictures of the tortured bodies of civilians who opposed the repressive regime, and he wrote to the authorities asking for help to put an end to the fear and oppression in which his parishioners lived. When the government was unresponsive, he began to reflect on the need for these people to organize to obtain redress and change their situation. He realized that the conservative tradition of the Church in Latin America, allied to the plutocracy, catering to the rich, and helping the poor solely through the distribution of alms to those most needy, merely served to perpetuate injustice. He felt that the poor and powerless had the right to try and alter their situation through self-help organizations, through education and community action. He also felt that the Church had an obligation through its leadership to assist this process in concrete ways.

His efforts to serve these parishioners offended not only the repressive government and the upper classes, but even his wealthy parishioners who felt the Church was undermining their privileges. When he baptized Indian babies in the same baptismal font as the privileged white babies, they were outraged. His support of lay Catholic self-help groups was attacked as socialist activism. And, when he stood in the pulpit and called for an end to the government's violence against opposition groups, he was shot down in broad daylight.

At his funeral, held on March 30, 1980 at the Cathedral, government troops opened fire on the overflow crowd. The massacre left 44 dead and hundreds wounded. Among the witnesses that day was Maryknoll lay missionary Jean Donovan.

A year later Jean Donovan, along with two Maryknoll nuns— Maura Clarke and Ita Ford, and Dorothy Kazel, an Ursuline sister, were abducted, raped and shot to death by National Guardsmen. The next day peasants discovered their bodies alongside an isolated road buried in a shallow grave. Everyone familiar with the case knew that these women were killed by National Guardsmen and that the murders were countenanced, if not actually ordered, by the government.[1] Yet, when the Pope visited El Salvador in 1983, he purposely refused to address the murder of his bishop, or the murders of Jean Donovan and the nuns. He pointedly said the purpose of the Church was to teach that Jesus is the Son of God and to provide spiritual counsel to the flock. Privately, he met with the priests and nuns in El Salvador and told them to discontinue their involvement with community self-help groups. He replaced the murdered Archbishop Romero with a conservative, giving him identical instructions in an effort to restore the Church to its former alliance with those in power—no matter how corrupt or complicit in organized violence—for which the Church was notorious a century before.

Nicaragua: The day before the Pope's visit to Managua in 1983, 17 members of a youth organization who had been murdered by Somoza's soldiers were buried after a memorial program in the same plaza where Pope John Paul II was to say Mass. It was hoped by most of the mothers and young people in attendance that the Pope would make some sympathetic remarks about the deaths of these teenagers. He did not. Instead he gave a sermon which demanded that the people of Nicaragua abandon their "untenable ideological commitments," and urged the bishops to be united. Previously, he had chastised Fr. Roberto Cardenal at the airport for his association with the farm workers' association, so a few in the congregation knew that no expression of unity with the people was likely to be forthcoming. Many others, however, believing the Pope was truly on the side of the people, began to chant: "A prayer for our dead" and "We want peace."[2] The Pope ignored them and finished his sermon. At the consecration, one of the mothers of the murdered boys broke in with a megaphone to say: "Holy Father, we beg you for a prayer for our loved ones who have been murdered."[3] The Pope not only did not offer that prayer but skipped the Lord's Prayer as well, with its traditional "sign of peace." He offered Communion to a few dignitaries, gave the last blessing, and exited.

Later the BBC announcer would call it one of the "most unusual Masses in this Pope's career." For President Daniel Ortega, who asked the Pope before leaving for a solid proposal for peace in Nicaragua, to say "one word which would strengthen the people," it was more than unusual. It was the turning away of this representative of the Prince of Peace from a clear opportunity to have an impact. To say that he left behind many alienated Catholics is an understatement.

It has been said by insiders that when the Pope asked what the people were shouting during the Mass ("Queremos paz!" We want peace!), he was told by one of his aides that it was of no importance, and that those calling out were Communists. With his own experience of Communism in Eastern Europe, this statement was like flashing a red cape before a bull. Not long after, the liberal bishops were replaced by conservatives as the Pope, encouraged by Ratzinger (who wrote a thesis on the subject), was shown alleged links between elements of liberation theology and Marxism. "The Pope began listening to those who were portraying liberation theology in caricatures—priests with guns, Marxists—and they just weren't accurate,"[4] said Dean Brackley, a theology professor at a Latin American Jesuit university. The following year, leading Brazilian liberation theologian Leonard Boff was ordered to Rome and sentenced to a year of "obsequious silence" by Cardinal Ratzinger's committee, during which time he was denied permission to publish or to teach publicly. He has since resigned from the Franciscan order.[5]

Preferential Option: It could easily have been otherwise, without Ratzinger's influence. Pope John Paul II was also familiar with the Solidarity Movement in Poland, which was far more similar to the farm organizations and rural artisan groups in El Salvador and Nicaragua than with Marxism. But the die had been cast and the Church abandoned two decades of social activism and the "preferential option for the poor" to return to the "benevolent absence" which characterized so much of Latin America's hierarchy in the years of the dictators.

The preferential option for the poor and vulnerable was a concept that had evolved in the early sixties and became part of the Church philosophy at the Conferences of Latin American Bishops in Medellín, Colombia (1968) and Puebla, Mexico (1979). Essentially it noted that there was a growing awareness of the poor's solidarity among themselves, their efforts to support one another, and their public demonstrations which, without recourse to violence, presented their own needs and rights in the face of the public authorities' inefficiency or corruption. "By virtue of her own evangelical duties," the bishops stated, "the Church must stand beside the poor, to discern the justice of their requests and to help satisfy them without losing sight of the common good."[6] The bishops went on to say that, "As followers of

Christ we are challenged to make a preferential option for the poor, namely, to create conditions for marginalized voices to be heard, to defend the defenseless, and to assess lifestyles, policies and social institutions in terms of their impact on the poor. The option for the poor does not mean pitting one group against another, but rather it calls us to strengthen the whole community by assisting those who are most vulnerable." [7]

Cardinal Ratzinger's Reversal: "An analysis of 'liberation theology'," wrote Cardinal Ratzinger in 1984, "reveals that it constitutes a fundamental threat to the faith of the Church." He goes on to discover "radically marxist (sic) positions" in those who teach the theology and, although he acknowledges that "no error could persist unless it contained a grain of truth…an error is all the more dangerous, the greater that grain of truth is."[8] The grain of truth, of course, is the mission of Christ and his apostles as defined by the Gospels, most notably by the Sermon on the Mount where Jesus clearly affirms the "option for the poor." Cardinal Ratzinger replies that this is an amalgam of a basic truth of Christianity and an un-Christian fundamental option, which is seductive and has the semblance of truth. "The Sermon on the Mount is indeed God taking sides with the poor," he writes. "But interpreting the poor in the sense of the marxist dialectic of history, and taking sides with them in the sense of class struggle, is a wanton attempt to portray as identical things that are contrary." While acknowledging the "irresistible logic of the liberation theologians," Cardinal Ratzinger suggests that this new interpretation of Christianity is tainted, that we should return to the "logic of faith, and present it as the logic of reality,"[9] and that theologians, priests, lay people and nuns cannot interpret God's word, only the Church herself has that authority.

The order to silence the liberation theologians which came shortly thereafter not only deprived professors of their jobs, priests of their most salient message to the poor, and removed bishops from their dioceses to be replaced by men who agreed with Cardinal Ratzinger, it also had a more deadly effect. It sent a message to the repressive regimes in Latin America that these people did not have the protection or support of the Church. Lay missionaries, nuns, priests, teachers, even aid workers were immediately seen as soft targets for the repressive regimes. One of the most brutal massacres which followed was the assault on the Central America University (UCA) in San Salvador. There, in the early hours of November 16, 1989, soldiers entered the Jesuit residence and assassinated the university president, Fr. Ignacio Ellacuria, and five other priests. Their cook Elba Ramos and her daughter Celina, who asked to stay the night for their own safety since soldiers had surrounded the campus, were also murdered.[10]

The murders of the Jesuit priests at the university sent a message to all those associated with liberation theology. With the withdrawal of Rome's support for their work, with the clear import of Cardinal Ratzinger's "Instruction" that this was a Marxist tainted movement, everyone working in Latin America outside official government channels was vulnerable. The priests at the university were teachers and scholars. Fr. Ellacuria, a Madrid native, was internationally known as an educator and was even friends with former U.N. ambassador Jean Kirkpatrick. In the words of Fr. Charles Beirne, S.J., "They were priests, not partisan politicians. They dealt with the *polis*, the poor, and they explored the ethical dimensions of the national reality. For this they were silenced."[11]

The Red Herring of Marxism: Jean Donovan, the lay missionary who was murdered along with the nuns in El Salvador, was the daughter of a Sikorsky aircraft engineer from Westport, Connecticut. Raised in relative affluence, she had a masters degree in business administration from Case Western Reserve, was a dedicated Catholic and a lifelong Republican.

Well on her way to a successful management career in Cleveland, in 1979 she volunteered though her local church to work at a mission in El Salvador with the organization Caritas, after hearing of the work of Bishop Romero and the desperate plight of the children in that country. Shortly after her arrival in Central America, her letters home began to note mounting evidence of the connection between U.S. policies and the violence in El Salvador.[12] With the election of Ronald Reagan in 1980 and his promise of a strong stand against "Communism" in Central America, she saw that the U.S. had effectively given the repressive regimes in that region exactly what they needed: a free hand to eliminate opposition, stifle worker organizations, and intimidate (or even eliminate) relief workers whose support of "the people" rather than "the government" could be interpreted as Marxist. "Things grew progressively worse in El Salvador after the U.S. election...The military believed they were given a blank check—no restrictions."[13]

The conflation of Catholic social work and Marxism by both governments had its effect. Reagan administration officials parroted the Salvadoran government's excuse for the rape-murders, saying that the women had "run a roadblock," and were "not just nuns but political activists." When the Donovan family approached the State Department for information regarding the apprehension of those responsible for the murder of their daughter, they were treated coolly and then with hostility. The U.S. government, which they had formerly believed in so strongly as a bastion of justice, now appeared allied with the forces of repression. Eventually they were told to stop bothering State Department officials. The final insult occurred when they received a bill from the State Department for $3,500 for the return of Jean's body.[14] Meanwhile, the head of the National Guard who was responsible for the murders, General Eugenio Vides Casanova, went on to become Minister of Defense under the U.S.-supported, "democratic" regime of José Napoleón Duarte. And thus the revolutionary era of the 80s came to an end in Central America.

What followed in the 90s was a retreat from activism on the part of the Catholic hierarchy, the replacement of hundreds of bishops by more conservative prelates, a ban on teaching liberation theology in the universities, the silencing of major Latin American theologians, and a slow retreat of the Church from social activism. In Central America, local organizations have since lost much of their initiative and support, and true democracy has disappeared to be replaced with neoliberal "show" democracy in which one of the two wealthiest candidates gets to take control of the government with the blessings of the U.S. Today, war-ravaged El Salvador and Nicaragua, as well as Guatemala, are worse off than they were fifty years ago, with more than half the population receiving less than the minimal daily food intake for sustenance, with high unemployment, war and hurricane-damaged infrastructure, skyrocketing illiteracy rates, juvenile crime waves, and hopelessness. The charitable soup kitchens and food baskets of 2009 are a far cry from the self-help groups, organized *campesinos*, trade unions, and health clinics that the Church help organize and support in the 1980s.

In South America (with Venezuela, Brazil and Uruguay being exceptions), most countries have surrendered their political autonomy to the IMF, the World Bank and corporate investors. In some of these countries, most notably Brazil, liberation theology has deepened and broadened, especially where it is apparent that only pastoral work can serve the poor whom the State and neoliberal policies have left behind.

143

In Venezuela, the vacuum left by the loss of an activist Church has been filled by the populism of President Chávez who, fueled by the U.S. premature "recognition" of his replacement during an unsuccessful coup attempt,[15] has created a war economy ("Avoid the U.S. Invasion, Pay Your Taxes") [16] while carefully distributing some of the oil largess to the most visible of the needy sectors.

Attempting to compete with the large numbers of poor who now flock to Christian evangelical churches where they can sing away their blues, praise the Lord, and hope for a better world after death, the new Pope (with the recruitment help of Opus Dei) has begun searching for young, good-looking, charismatic priests who can run the same type of operation with the Catholic imprimatur. They have had some limited successes especially with youth camps and rallies in which young people gather in open fields to attend what appear to be Christian versions of sixties rock concerts. Pope Benedict's call for a new "evangelical mission" in recent communications to Latin America seems to be basically this: a removal of the Church from any real effort to work for social justice in Latin America and a decision to compete not for souls, but for audiences in a new evangelical movement, where hymns, invocations of the Holy Spirit and shouted amens and alleluias will provide an other-worldly escape from reality, and where religion will finally become, as Marx so prophetically noted, merely an opiate of the people. The genuine irony is, of course, that liberation theology and the option for the poor which Cardinal Ratzinger denigrated as

Marxist, was a clear and powerful alternative to Marxism, and, unlike populism and the militarism which will likely follow as current regimes fail to deliver social justice, it continues to be the best hope of empowering people to change their lives, to create grass roots democratic movements, and to form safe, self-sufficient and prosperous communities.

NOTES:

1. There are numerous sources which recount in detail what happened to Jean Donovan and the three nuns. Among the best is the recent book: *Salvador Witness: The Life and Calling of Jean Donovan* by Ann Carrigan. Obis Books. Maryknoll, NY. 2005 from which some of this background is drawn.

2. From "The 1983 Visit of Pope John Paul II to Nicaragua" by Katherine Hoyt. http://www.hartford_hwp.com/archives/47/030.html This is the text of a letter written by Hoyt to her parents a few days after the Pope's visit to Managua. It was later posted on the web because of the authoritative nature of the account. Hoyt is the national coordinator of the Nicaragua Network Education Fund.

3. *Ibid.* The quotes which follow are all from Hoyt's account.

4. The Dean Brackley quote is from "Part of the Flock Felt Abandoned by the Pope" by Cris Kraul and Henry Chu. L.A. Times, April 10, 2005. http://www.latimes.com/news/nationworld/world/la-fg-libtheology10apr10,0,4626986.story

5. *Ibid.,* p. 2.

6. From "An Introduction to the Principles of Catholic Social Thought. University of Notre Dame." http://www.centerforsocialconcerns.nd.edu/mission/cst/cst4.shtml

7. *Ibid.,* p.1

8. From "Preliminary Notes to Liberation Theology" by Joseph Cardinal Ratzinger which preceded the "Instruction" of Fall, 1984. http://www.christendom-awake.org/pages/retzinger/liberationtheol.htm

9. Ratzinger, *op. cit.,* Sec. III, "Central Concepts of Liberation Theology."

10. *Ibid.,* pp.7-8.

11. This information is from the Religious Task Force on Central America located at UCA, where the Jesuits were murdered. See "Martyrs of the University of Central America." http://www.rtfcam.org/martyrs/UCA/UCA.htm

12. "Ordinary People Made Extraordinary" by Fr. Charles Beirne, S.J. http://www.companysj.com/w171/ordinary.html

13. From "Jean Donovan: Except for the Children." http://www.rftcam.org/martyrs/women/jean_donovan.htm

14. *Ibid.* Quote is attributed to her mother, Patricia.

15. *Ibid.,* p. 4.

16. In an April 13, 2002 editorial following the attempted coup, the *New York Times* declared, "Venezuelan democracy is no longer threatened by a would-be dictator." The *Times* went on to explain that Chávez was "forced down by the military and replaced by a business leader." Three days later, the *Times* offered a slightly apologetic retraction: "Mr. Chávez has been such a divisive and demagogic leader that his departure last week drew applause at home and in Washington. That reaction, which we shared, overlooked the undemocratic manner in which he was removed. Forcibly unseating a democratic leader, no matter how badly he has performed, is never something to cheer."

17. This was on a banner viewed by the author near the Caracas airport on October 20, 2005.

CHAPTER XI: DISMANTLING THE CENTRAL AMERICAN GANGS AND RECOVERING A LOST GENERATION

Guatemala City, Guatemala

Carlos, my driver, was a former federal policeman. He weighed a good two hundred pounds and was well over six feet. He was assigned to me by a local businessman I knew in Guatemala City, after I explained that I wanted to visit some areas where I could see gang activity. When we arrived at the *tianguis* or local market, he pulled over the Ford Explorer and opened the glove compartment. He unclipped his automatic from his belt, and put it inside along with his wallet. "Take a few bills out of your wallet and then put it inside the glove box as well," he said. Then he locked the glove compartment.

"If it's so dangerous here," I asked, "why don't you take your gun?"

"Because kids operate in packs of five or six. Twelve and thirteen-year olds. They rush you and take whatever you have, and are gone before you even have time to react. That's how quick they are. And we don't need another automatic weapon on the streets."

Later we discussed the problems of delinquency, gang aggression, and law enforcement in the city. In the past, many of these delinquents were simply taken by the police into alleys where they were beaten severely and then released. Now, with complaints from human rights groups, the police are more constrained. If there are clear indications of gang affiliation such as tattoos, scarves, jackets, they are often arrested and sent to an adult prison facility. If there are not, as is often the case with the youngest offenders, the police rely on rogue cops or private enforcers to take them off the street, sometimes permanently. Lack of juvenile facilities, few police officers, serious adult unemployment and crime, have ironically led to worse abuses (even murders) of young people than had occurred prior to the intervention of human rights groups. Still, for most young people roaming the mean streets of Guatemala, Honduras, Nicaragua, El Salvador and the Dominican Republic is much safer than going to prison or even awaiting trial in jail.

Social Cleansing by Fire

Prison massacres are commonplace in Central America and juveniles are often the target. In the Dominican Republic where the prisons are 215% over intended capacity, a fire in March, 2005 killed 136 inmates and left many more with life-threatening injuries.[1] In May, 2004 in San Pedro Sula, Honduras, a fire killed 103; in April a year earlier 79 inmates were killed in a prison fire. Nor have the prisoners further south escaped what seems like a plague of inmates' deaths from

Maracaibo, Venezuela, where 100 inmates were killed, to Cardiru, Brazil, where a similar tragedy led to an exposé documentary.

"They wanted to leave us to die, one Honduran inmate told *La Prensa*.[2] "We heard them say, 'Let's leave these pieces of garbage to die,'" said this witness in the San Pedro Sula jail, where the victims, mostly gang members, either suffocated or were burned alive in their cells.

After the Dominican fire killing 136, General Juan Ramon de la Cruz, a prison official, reluctantly acknowledged that most of the prisons operated under a system of corruption and privilege.[3] It is clearly understood that many of the guards (often demobilized military and laid-off police) are corrupt, compromised or just plan frightened. They often desert the prison interior during a crisis, such as a fire, to the safety of the walls, leaving the prisoners trapped.

History of Latino Gangs

In recent years the appearance of Central American gangs in the United States has caused law enforcement authorities, even Homeland Security, grave concern. Conservative groups have blamed the porous Mexican border. Al Valdez, an investigator from the Orange County D.A.'s office, calls them a "South American import."[4] The Heritage Foundation and MILNET, two conservative think tanks, trace them a bit more precisely to those "displaced by Central American civil wars in the 1980s and to illegals that have been deported from the U.S. and then returned."[5]

However, neither Mr. Valdez with his "South American import" nor MILNET with its "civil wars" is quite accurate. The major gangs are located in Central, not South, America. In addition, conservative commentators either minimize or distort the nature of U.S. involvement in Central America which contributed significantly to the problem.[6] U.S. intervention in Central America in the 1980s to support corrupt militarist regimes and destroy popular resistance created millions of refugees, many of them children. Thousands ended up on the streets of L.A., Miami, Chicago and other U.S. cities. Often without a father figure, inured to violence from years of warfare, distrustful of authority, they joined street gangs already in existence or formed those of their own. Some were incarcerated in U.S. prisons where they learned even more about gang solidarity before being deported back to El Salvador, Nicaragua, Guatemala and Honduras. Many of these were peasant kids who had no idea of what a gang was until they were "educated" on the mean streets of East L.A. So, to a large extent, the gang phenomenon is a North American export.

When I arrived in Guadalajara in 1988, for example, there was no graffiti on any of the buildings. It was unthinkable. Graffiti, tattoos, gang logos and jackets were something seen on TV shows from the United States. However, in the past decade, with the return of deportees, graffiti has become commonplace in Mexico and in most of

Central America as well, carrying with it the desecration of churches and colonial buildings, destroying the 500 year old ambience of historical districts.

Most sources agree that the major gangs which operate in Latin America today are ones which originated in the U.S. or were copied from existing U.S. gangs. Readers are familiar with predominately white gangs such as the Aryan Brotherhood and the Hells Angels. There are also black gangs such as the Crips and the Bloods, and the Black Muslims (which, though officially a religion, operates as a gang in most U.S. prisons). One of the oldest Latino gangs is the Mexican Mafia which was formed at the juvenile correctional facility in Tracy, California in the 1950s. It was originally composed of "Homies" who lived south of Bakersfield. They went on to become the most powerful in the prison system, eventually recruiting from the neighborhoods of East L.A. and throughout the Southwest.

The Norteños (aka *Nuestra Familia*) were formed at Folsom prison in the 1960s, mainly as a way to protect Latino inmates inside who came from areas north of Bakersfield. The gang members tattooed themselves with the Roman Numeral XIV for 14, the 14th letter of the alphabet "N" for Norte, or with four dots on the hand. Another southern California group, the 18th street gang, formed in the Rampart District of Los Angeles, has members who are tattooed with XVIII (or 666, whose total is 18). This gang is very powerful and is reported to have over 20, 000 members.

A rival gang MS-13, better known as Mara Salvatrucha (from *Mara* or "gang" and *salvatrucha*, slang for "smart Salvadoran"), is associated with southern families of Mexican national gangs and has grown to be the most notorious in recent years. They often have a 13 tattoo (M for Mara) and the S also stands for Sur or Sureño (South).[7]

Many of these gangs have loose alliances with other chapters and with other gangs as well. Often those associated with the Mexican Mafia are called La Eme (The M) and have known to have formed alliances for mutual protection with black gangs, and even with the Aryan Brotherhood.

After the U.S.-sponsored wars in Nicaragua and El Salvador (using Honduras as a training ground for Contras), many residents fled Central America, especially those that had the funds to do so, or widows with children who could claim asylum status. Thousands of young people ended up in the ethnic neighborhoods of Chicago, Miami and Los Angeles in the 1980s. Many joined gangs for reasons of solidarity, mutual protection, and camaraderie. Others were induced to join by threats or violence to them or their families. Those who got into trouble were sent to juvenile detention centers such as Tracy (known to young inmates as "Gladiator School") where they were initiated into the violence for which these gangs have become notorious.

In the past 25 years, thousands have been deported, including some during the height of Hurricane Jeanne which cost the lives of 4,000 people in Central America and the Caribbean and was far more disastrous (with embarrassingly less relief from international organizations, including the U.S.) than Hurricane Katrina. If Rev. Jesse Jackson's remarks about the effect of race and class on the tardiness of response and the quality of relief efforts after Katrina was considered inappropriate by CNN news interviewers, it was an obvious truism to those in Honduras, Haiti and the Dominican Republic where the catastrophic death and destruction of Hurricane Jeanne were not even reported in the U.S. press.

Armed and Dangerous vs. Young and Feckless

Once back in their home countries, with easy access to weapons left behind by U.S.-sponsored forces,[8] these young delinquents became a significant threat to the security and stability of the region. While estimates of gang membership in Central America have varied from 30,000 to 150,000, the following data are the regional police estimates of gang membership: 14,000 in Guatemala, 10,500 in El Salvador, 36,000 in Honduras, 1,000 in Nicaragua, 2,600 in Costa Rica and 1,380 in Panama.[9] However, when you consider that Salvadoran security forces have detained more than 20,000 people on gang-related charges since July 2003, it appears that most, if not all, of these estimates are conservative. In addition, they do not take into account the loosely-organized bands of teens and pre-teens such as those operating in the streets of Guatemala City, who claim no specific affiliation.

155

The violent potential of some of these gang members cannot be underestimated. In Honduras, twenty-three passengers were killed on a public bus apparently in retaliation for prison deaths earlier in the year.[10] In Nicaragua, presidential candidates could not campaign without a safe-conduct bribe to the gangs in many neighborhoods.[11] Similar safe-conducts are required to shop in many of the open-air markets in Guatemala and El Salvador. The de-activation of the Contras, and the peace accords in Central America which led to the withdrawal of U.S. advisors and Contra mercenaries, have left behind thousands of rounds of ammunition, grenades, land mines, and automatic rifles available at bargain basement prices. The budget-slashing and belt-tightening which Central American economies have undergone in the decades following these U.S.-sponsored wars has left governments without the funds to support education, youth facilities, juvenile courts or detention centers, or even a professional military. Without sufficient police personnel or proper investigative and prosecutorial procedures in the courts, those responsible for crimes are often not arrested, or if arrested, not successfully prosecuted because of lack of witnesses or evidence. Thus it is that some of the most dangerous gang members, financed by drugs and arms' sales, are able to intimidate witnesses, bribe police, and elude prosecution.

On the other hand, younger gang members, even street children who are often "wannabes," or simply pre-teens and teens hanging out with friends, are often picked up, assaulted, incarcerated without due process and left to rot in jails. Others are killed in sweeps through barrios by death squads called *Sombra Negra* or Black Shadow, composed of private police paid by landowners, ex-military thugs, and rogue cops.

A *Mano Dura* (or Heavy Hand) policy on the part of the Central American presidents, including Manuel Zelaya, a right wing autocrat, has led to the round-up of thousands of "suspected" gang members (judged usually by tattoos, the barrios in which they are found, jackets or other clothing) and their incarceration in crowded jails without benefit of trial, where many are murdered or left to die in unexplained fires. Demobilized soldiers and private security forces also operate within the region to take out suspected gang members vigilante-style in alleys, unlit streets, and remote barrios. In Honduras, "social cleansing" has resulted in the deaths since 1998 of almost over 2,300 youngsters[12] who were accused of no crime but suspected of having gang affiliations. The young, the feckless, the homeless street children are often easy targets for the self-styled "social cleansers" who would not have the *cojones* to take on veteran gang members.

Causes of Continued Growth of Gangs

While it is important not to underestimate the causes that initiated the rise of the gangs in Central America and the responsibility of the U.S. for its genesis, it is equally important to note that the growth of gangs has continued exponentially with no encouragement from U.S.

foreign policy of the past twenty-five years. The underlying causes for the growth are many and I will enumerate some of them here, first, to show how complex the problem is, so it becomes clear that more police power is not the answer. And second, to show how the U.S. government, private groups, international corporations, and NGOs can help citizens of these countries wrest control of their communities from the gangs which are now effectively holding them hostage.

I should note in passing that the people most affected by the gangs are the poor and lower middle class. In all of these countries, the politicos, the professionals, the upper class landowners and military elite all live in guarded compounds with trained dogs, security forces, alarms, and 24-hour police patrols. It is the poor and working classes who are the victims as usual, housed in dangerous tenements or in shacks in unpaved and unlighted barrios, where the police dare not enter at night and where fear is a constant companion. It was poor working folks who lost their lives on the bus in Honduras, not wealthy citizens safely ensconced in their Mercedes and Land Rovers.

Some of the causes of gang violence do stem from the conflicts of the eighties with the loss of fathers in war, loss of respect for the homeland because of political corruption, alienation from cultural and religious restraint, withdrawal of U.S. support after significant damage to infrastructure, discarded weapons and land mines, immigration and deportation. However, for the latest generation of gang members, factors closer to home are also worth noting:

*A tradition of institutionalized violence which is mirrored in the families.

*Chronic unemployment exacerbated by neoliberal policies.

*Cutbacks in social services and education due to IMF and World Bank imperatives.

*Loss of credibility of authority figures.

*A decline in respect for the Catholic Church after murders of priests and nuns by government forces and the replacement of liberation theology bishops by conservative clergy.

*Substance abuse and the prevalence of drug money.

*The attraction of violence in the culture and the media.

*Access to inexpensive weapons.

*Impediments to employment because of juvenile arrests.

*Negative influences of the U.S. on the culture.

*The natural inclination of youth for solidarity, and for feelings of security and belonging.

*The breakdown of family units due to relocation (neoliberal "flexibility of labor").

*Scarcity of educational opportunities and paucity of trained teachers.

*Lack of recreational alternatives to street activities.

I mentioned the U.S. involvement as one of the primary causes at the beginning, not to assign blame but to indicate our responsibility to this region. Gang activity was an "unintended consequence" of U.S.-

sponsored war and our subsequent withdrawal without even minimum efforts to restore the infrastructures of these countries. In addition, the gangs were indeed a U.S. export, as we have seen. It seems to me that acceptance of that historical fact should give us the public will to help our neighbors to the south address the problem. Here are some of the initiatives I propose:

Tentative Solutions to the Problem

1.   International corporations such as Coca-Cola, Honda, Liggett and Myers, Disney, Monsanto, IBM, Bayer, GE, Ford, Procter and Gamble, Continental Airlines, Air America, Westinghouse, Bell South, Hertz, Hilton, Crowne Plaza, Phillips, GM, Hewlett-Packard and dozens of others, market and sell their merchandise and services in these countries, while utilizing the lower labor costs. They should acknowledge their civic responsibility to their hosts and provide corporate sponsorship to youth leagues and football clubs. Local police should be encouraged to form police benevolent leagues as they have in the U.S. and provide the young boys with Golden Gloves and other healthy activities as an alternative to violence and to street life.

2.   U.S.A.I.D. funds should be used to support teacher training centers, and international educators at American Schools in the region should be required, as part of their contracts, to mentor local teachers.

3.   U.S. and Canadian law enforcement, besides establishing a

method for data sharing within the region and continentally, should also provide expertise of the kind that has curtailed the growth of gangs in such U.S. and Canadian cities as Miami, Chicago, Seattle, Vancouver and Toronto, and offered decent alternatives to the youth there. Department of Justice grants to Homies Unidos and other gang prevention and rehabilitation groups would help them share their expertise and establish similar groups in Central America.

4. International leadership by the World Bank, the International Monetary Fund, advisors to NAFTA, CAFTA, the OAS and related organizations within the region should encourage national employment programs, social security, worker protection, minimum wage, clean water, and public control of utilities as well as forgiveness of external debt to these countries, to give them an opportunity to establish some minimalist caretaking capabilities for their poorest populations.

5. A fresh recognition by both the U.S. government and the international business community, which have been pushing global and continental agendas in the Americas, that corporate profits and free trade cannot come at the expense of workers' rights, destruction of the environment, and imposition of police states to handle social problems incurred by vast numbers of young people abandoned by economies which have rendered them superfluous, while enriching their leaders and their trading partners to the north.

6.   A planned moratorium on gun sales and firearm possession in Central American countries arrived at by a regional treaty which begins with (a) elimination of unrestricted advertising of guns in the local media[13] and (b) collection of unregistered guns with a cash and amnesty incentive, and (c) culminates in a policy similar to Great Britain's zero tolerance program.

7.   A planned use of 5% of remittances from Central Americans working abroad, coupled with matching national government funds, to be invested in community rebuilding, and in supporting local schools, free clinics, and other social projects to be determined by local democratically-elected committees.

8.   Action groups to support substance abuse recovery programs and share educational initiatives for young people with drug and alcohol abuse problems, offer assistance to children of alcoholics and drug addicts, and provide family counseling. Each of these should be coordinated from the start with resources from AA International and NA International.

9.   The Washington Office on Latin America and the Interamerican Coalition for Prevention of Youth Violence[14] has each urged a comprehensive policy that invests in both long-term and short-term youth violence prevention programs, and in rehabilitation programs for those who wish to leave gangs. That is the last piece in this comprehensive package.

A few years ago I visited Chicago on a book tour and accompanied Police Commander Moe Daley on his rounds in the Pilsen/Little Village District which used to be notorious for gang activity and crime. He showed me how their community had been revitalized by small business loans, by residents painting and repairing dilapidated houses with materials supplied by a local foundation. He showed me how the city helped the residents by blocking off streets with small and tasteful concrete barriers to traffic and creating safe blocks, how they supported local traditions and heritage in the form of a Mexican museum, Latino bookstores, Spanish language newspapers, a *panadería*, and through city-wide business and citizen support for Cristo Rey High School where the students earned their tuition by working one day a week for local businesses. Here was creative law enforcement and civic leadership. Commander Daley's officers on the beat knew all the gang members and ex-gang members by name, had them in a data base, had often made interventions to get them into AA or NA, find them jobs—and when they had to, arrest them for possession, burglary, or other crimes with the active support of the citizenry. But both he and his officers had a larger goal than just controlling the gangs. Their goal was to create a safe and prosperous community where their children could be educated, have opportunities, and yet continue to live with the traditions and values that their families had inherited long before they moved to Chicago. This is the vision we have to share with Central America.

The United States government, educators and business people working in Central America, students, North American law enforcement personnel working with their Central American colleagues can all play a role, not only in preventing the spread of youth violence, but in reversing the trend entirely. All that is necessary is the will.[15] Without it, Central America will become more dangerous than Afghanistan, our borders will be increasingly threatened, and the most valuable resource of the Americas—its young people—will become objects of fear, chaos and destruction, instead of the young leaders and productive citizens they have the potential to be.

NOTES

1. "Dominican Republic: Prison Fire Highlights Abuses" by James T. Kimer. *NACLA Report on the Americas.* Vol. 38 No. 6, May/June 2005, p. 47.

2. "Guards accused over Honduras fire." *BBC News.* Tuesday, 18 May 2004. http://news.bbc.co.uk/2/hi/americas/3724221.stm

3. Kimer, James. T., *op.cit,* p. 47.

4. "A South American Import" by Investigator Al Valdez. *National Alliance of Gang Investigators' Associations.* http://www.nagia.org/mara_salvatrucha.htm

5. *MILNET Brief.* http://www.milnet.com/mex-nat.html

6. See "North American Transnational Youth Gangs: Breaking the Chains of Violence" by Stephen Johnson and David Muhlhausen, Ph.D. Heritage Foundation. http://www.heritage.org/Research/UrbanIssues/bg1834.cfm

This otherwise comprehensive and accurate analysis is marred by misleading statements including one which characterizes the violence in El Salvador in the 1980s as "a 12 year civil war between communist guerillas and a fledgling democratic government," and the U.S. interventions in Nicaragua, Guatemala and Honduras as "helping to end communist insurgencies."

In El Salvador the U.S. supported a repressive militaristic regime; in Honduras it used that country as a base to train the Contras for their invasion of Nicaragua. In Nicaragua the U.S. fought in support of a dictator against a popular socialist movement. In Guatemala the CIA overthrew a democratically-elected president, resulting in violence which spanned four decades and resulted in the death of a hundred thousand civilians. Moreover, U.S. action in Nicaragua, including using the drug-money-funded Contras, and the mining of the harbor and Lake Nicaragua, were condemned by the World Court as state terrorist activities.

To ignore all of this and to purposely misstate the U.S. role in the region in Reagan-like language which has been discredited by the rest of the world, is to minimize the degree of U.S. responsibility for conditions in Central America today. It is to ignore as well, now that our attention is on the Middle East, the wreckage we have left behind which contributes to the problem of gang violence.

That said, the research of Johnson and Muhlhausen support my contention that the Central American gang violence is a U.S. export, noting that the Salvatruchas showed up as deportees in El Salvador in 1993 and Calle 18 members appeared in the region in 1996. This also accords with the observations of government officials in Central America.

7. For more information on the history, composition and idiosyncrasies of gangs in the U.S. visit http://KnownGangs.com or review the concise and largely accurate summaries on the MILNET site above.

8. "An Anatomy of Violence in El Salvador" by Joaquín M. Chávez. *NCLA Report on the Americas*. Vol. 37 No. 6, May/June 2004, pp. 31-37.

9. "Central America's Uneasy Disarmament" by Tim Rogers. *NACLA Report on the Americas.* Vol. 39 No. 1, July/August 2005, pp. 12-14.

10. "Gunman Killed 23 in Honduras Bus Attack." *China Daily*. Dec. 24, 2004. http://www.chinadaily.com.cn/english/doc.2004-12/24/content_403134.htm Also "Two more suspects arrested in Honduras bus attack." *Washington Post.* Dec. 26, 2004. http://washingtonpost.com/wp-dyn/articles/A6002-2004Dec25.html

11. I was in Managua and witnessed most of this gang activity during the presidential campaigning. In addition, the Bolaños rally (that of the winning presidential candidate in 2002) is wonderfully described in Marc Cooper's article "The Lost Revolution" from *Mother Jones.* Sept./Oct., 2001, pp. 71-77.

12. Rogers, James T., *op. cit.*, p. 14

13. Chávez, Joaquín, M., *op. cit.*, p. 37.

14. The entire text of the recent Field Conference on Central American Youth Gang Violence is available at the excellent site maintained by the Washington Office on Latin America. See http://www.wola.org/gangs/gangs/htm

15. There are excellent resources available on prevention programs and opportunities for readers who wish to become more actively involved. Please visit the site for the Washington Office on Latin America for more information. http://www.wola.org

CHAPTER XII: A CURE FOR HISTORICAL AMNESIA - How Latinos Can Remind Us Who We Really Are.

"The past is never dead. It's not even past."
—William Faulkner

Based on flimsy intelligence, which was then cynically manipulated to prove just cause for a preemptive war, the United States attacked in force. Its superior armaments overwhelmed the enemy. The U.S. press jubilantly supported the invasion and subsequent occupation, praising the troops as liberators. Though the U.S. suffered losses, they were minimal compared to those sustained by the enemy and by the civilian population. However, as the months passed, the occupation began to seem interminable, and the local government, set up with support of the occupying forces, appeared unreliable and ineffective. It was suggested by some generals and congressional observers that the country appeared "unfit for democracy." Sound familiar? No, it is not Iraq in 2006; it was Cuba in 1898.

Remember the Maine!

On February 15, 1898, the battleship *Maine* exploded in Havana Bay, killing 260 U.S. sailors and Marines. Intelligence sources, largely at the service of William Randolph Hearst, supplied the government with evidence that a mine had been placed in the hold of the ship by agents of the Spanish government. A sketch showing the location of the device and the wires linking it to the ship's engine room was also provided. On April 25th, President McKinley asked Congress to declare war against Spain for this terrorist act.

Six weeks later, a report to Congress concluded that there was no Spanish involvement. In fact, it was even suggested (and later proven by a U.S. admiral) that there was no explosive device at all. The explosion was caused by the spontaneous combustion of the ship's coal bins, a relatively common problem in those days.

Facts then, as now, had little relevance to the Administration. The war had begun and would be seen through to its conclusion. It gave U.S. youth opportunities to be heroes in a war which was relatively easy to win against an outgunned army and a negligible navy. U.S. torture of prisoners and other abuses were excused by previous Spanish atrocities. Historical references to the Spanish Inquisition and the decadent but still dangerous Roman Catholic religion were rampant in the U.S. press.

Intolerance and jingoism were on the loose, and repressive immigration laws and racial invective were as common in the streets as they were in public discourse. Nations who criticized the U.S. were accused of being anti-American, as were domestic critics such as philosopher William James, who cautioned his fellow countrymen to be more thoughtful. He had his work cut out for him. U.S. books and tracts, many published by religious organizations, painted the Spanish race as lawless, sneaky, lazy, venal and treacherous. The Roman Catholic religion was seen not only as inimical to democracy, but also as the antithesis of the spirit of Protestant free enterprise.

But, if the Spanish were unfit to rule, it did not mean that the local population, *mestizos* and Indians, were thought any more suited to the task. Considered even less capable of self-government without the heavy hand of U.S. occupiers, they became the beneficiaries of a century of advisors, colonial surrogates, businessmen, bankers and managers who settled in the country, micro-managed its productive resources, and influenced elections so that the United States would always have preferential trade agreements, cheap natural resources to import, and a controlled little colony where wealthy tourists could gamble and have cheap sex. Best of all, the U.S. could install a permanent military base at Guantanamo Bay where it could control the Caribbean.

One of the heroes of the "splendid little war" with Spain was Teddy Roosevelt, who persuaded his friends in the Administration (where he was Undersecretary of the Navy) to give him a lieutenant colonel's commission in the cavalry. He then gathered together an all-volunteer regiment which he called the "Rough Riders," mostly veterans of the Indian wars. His subsequent "cavalry charge up San Juan Hill" became part of a legend that is still in every U.S. history textbook in public schools. In fact, there was no mounted charge up San Juan Hill. The cavalry assault, such as it was, took place at a smaller preliminary embankment called Kettle Hill, after which the riders dismounted and met up with several other regiments and artillery which overwhelmed the Spanish by superior numbers and armaments. Indeed, not only was the battle insignificant in terms of personal risk and bravery but, according to Stephen Crane, author of *The Red Badge of Courage* and a reporter at the battle, several of the Rough Riders panicked during the fracas.

Nevertheless, the heroic lieutenant colonel went on to become president of the United States, and commenced a plan for hemispheric imperialism which would be unprecedented in the annals of recorded history. He would also wage war without benefit of Congressional approval. His "legal" justification for this dramatic incrementation of executive power was what is now known as "the Roosevelt Corollary" to the Monroe Doctrine.

The Monroe Doctrine stated essentially that any foreign power interfering in the affairs of any Latin American or Caribbean republic would be considered an aggression against the United States which could then, without further ado, enter that country and eliminate the interfering party. The Roosevelt Corollary expanded the writ even further. Citing the lack of leadership and inexperience with democratic principles among Latin American governments, Roosevelt proposed that the United States, when it perceived weakness or instability in a Latin American or Caribbean republic, could enter that country to resolve the problem, including eliminating the existing government and replacing it with another more suitable! Nor was this any empty threat. For depending on whose statistics you include, the United States has invaded or otherwise forcibly interfered in Latin American countries over 80 times in the past 150 years (U.S. Department of State records), or more than 120 times (according to Venezuelan president Hugo Chávez). The historical truth is closer to the Chávez estimate, since the State Department does not count clandestine interference or invasions through the instrumentality of others (such as the Bay of Pigs where exiled Cubans under U.S. direction acted as the invading force).

Let's Make a New Country!

Once Roosevelt became president he also resurrected the idea of an intercontinental canal. The logical place was the Isthmus of Nicaragua. However, volcanic activity in that country scared off investors. The Isthmus of Panama in the Republic of Colombia was more suitable. Some of the initial digging had already been done by a French company which later abandoned the project. The only problem was that the Colombian government was not interested in having the U.S. military establish a base on its territory, displacing residents and engaging in a massive dig, without a number of reassurances and agreements which Roosevelt was reluctant to give. So he colluded with a French undercover agent in Panama City by the name of Buneau-Varilla to organize a rebel force with the intent of getting Panama to secede from Colombia.

When the rebel forces attacked the municipal buildings at Colón and Panama City, Roosevelt had a fleet of ten gunships standing offshore ready to fire on civilian populations and destroy their cities unless the Colombian officials surrendered. They quickly capitulated. Ninety minutes later, the President recognized the rebels as the legitimate government of the new "Republic of Panama." "I took the Canal Zone and let Congress debate," Roosevelt quipped when he invited the French agent to a Washington hotel to draft the Panamanian constitution. The agent's wife, meanwhile, designed and sewed the Panamanian flag at the couple's new home in Highland Falls, N.Y.

Latin America now had a new republic, thanks to the United States. Of course, the people of Colombia were not consulted, and the "democratic institutions and values" of which the United States was so proud at home and ostensibly sought to promote abroad were a bit bruised.

And those preemptive invasions keep coming!

In the Dominican Republic, when that country was on the edge of bankruptcy and unable to pay foreign loans, Roosevelt sent the Marines and U.S. customs agents to Santo Domingo to take over the country's finances. With the Great White Fleet firmly in place in the Caribbean, the President wasted no time in enforcing his famous Corollary. Military interventions in Nicaragua and Honduras followed quickly, as the Marines moved in to protect U.S. mining and fruit companies. President Wilson would follow suit in his presidency with interventions in Haiti, the Dominican Republic, Mexico and the Philippines. The policy of armed intervention would continue in El Salvador where, under Hoover, the U.S. founded a military academy which spawned a brace of dictators and one of the most brutal and repressive militaries in the hemisphere.

When a reporter at the World's Fair in Flushing Meadows, N.Y. noted that Anastasio Somoza the dictator of Nicaragua was in attendance, and observed that he was a brutal leader, known for torture and even murder of the opposition, Franklin Roosevelt replied, "Yes, he is a son of a bitch. But he's our son of a bitch!" The new Roosevelt administration, concerned with economic recovery and the war with Germany and Japan, was willing to tolerate many sons of bitches as "allies," regardless of what happened to the citizens of these countries south of the border.

Eisenhower presided over the forced removal of the first democratic regime in Guatemala because it appeared too populist to suit the CIA. Later, Nixon gave his personal support to dictators in Nicaragua and El Salvador and to a brutal military regime in Guatemala known for the murders of tens of thousands of indigenous people. When his motorcade was stoned by students during his visit to Latin America, the folks back home were stunned. The public had little or no idea of how our policies in Latin America had destroyed lives, toppled legitimate governments, and made the few young people not starving to death cynical and distrustful of Washington.

Few presidents would surpass Ronald Reagan, however, who sponsored invasions of El Salvador, Nicaragua and Honduras, illegally diverted funds to finance reactionary forces, created a massive propaganda scheme to paint leftist rebels as pawns of the Soviets, ignored the murders of Catholic priests and nuns by government forces, and violated U.N. sanctions by mining Nicaraguan harbors and parklands for which the U.S. was condemned by the World Court. Even today, Nicaraguan children can be found missing an arm or a leg from landmines we left behind.

The problem is those Mexicans!

Today, U.S. intervention continues in Iraq at the cost of billions of dollars and thousands of lives. But the Congress and U.S. citizens are diverted from this legitimate concern by the likes of rabble rousers such as Lou Dobbs and Bill O'Reilly, the moral equivalents of "yellow journalist" William Randolph Hearst.

One would think, by listening to them, that the terrorists responsible for 9/11 were Mexicans who crossed our southern borders. They are spoken of as "illegal aliens" rather than undocumented workers, these people whose land was conquered and then confiscated in, according to Ulysses S. Grant, the "most unjust war ever waged by a stronger nation against a weaker one."

Two-fifths of Mexican territory passed to the United States as a result of the war with Mexico in 1846-48, one half if one includes Texas. It was one of the largest territorial conquests of any war in history adding one third to the land mass of the U.S. Yet it is the least known, the least discussed of any U.S. war, and it appears only in a few sentences under "Western Expansion" in most U.S. history texts. It raised the U.S. to First World status, gave it the ports of San Francisco, San Diego and Los Angeles, provided a western land route across the country, millions of acres of arable land, and invaluable deposits of gold and silver. Meanwhile, it deprived Mexico of half of its territory and reduced its citizens to Third World status.

Now in the 21st century, victims of economic exploitation and unfair competition, their land taken over by banks because their farmers are unable to compete with U.S. agricultural subsidies, their jobs lost due to unfair competition by conglomerates such as Wal-Mart which have forced small businesses into bankruptcy, their rivers polluted and their lands rendered arid due to environmental disasters caused by U.S. *maquiladoras*, they are victims of policies which have made Latin America the "dirty backyard" of the U.S. Now, when these "Americans" try to return to their ancestral lands in California, New Mexico and Arizona, they are treated like criminals. No mention is made of the hundreds of thousands of Eastern Europeans, Russians, Irish, Poles, Vietnamese, Cambodians, Canadians, Australians, Iranians, Saudis, Indians and Pakistanis who overstay their visas and are literally the "illegal aliens" in the country. Nor is mention made of the hundreds of thousands of Guatemalan, Nicaraguan, Salvadoran and Honduran refugees, the children of victims of our invasions and support for brutal repression in the 1980s, who "pass as Mexicans" and enter the United States illegally each year.

More Mexicans have fought and died in Iraq than any other nationality per capita.

The history of the United States' wars of intervention is an area in which the public is essentially illiterate. This is why its citizens are so easily distracted at this crucial time, and so easily led into a public discourse unworthy of them. What is even sadder is that the largest single contingent of Hispanics currently fighting in Iraq is made up of Mexicans and Mexican-Americans. According to journalist John Ross, there were 110,000 of them fighting in February of 2005. Called "green-card troops" and by some the "poverty draft," they were all actively recruited by the U.S. Army.

Between 31,000 and 37,000 of the 130,000 Hispanic troops currently in Iraq are non-citizens of the United States. While Latinos make up 12.5 percent of the U.S. population, they account for 17.5 percent of the front line forces. Of the first 1,000 combat deaths in Iraq, over 120 were Latino and 70 of them were Mexicans. (Source: *New Internationalist*. May, 2005, p. 8).

The large number of non-citizen Mexican troops, brothers-in-arms with the almost 100,000 Mexican-American citizens in the Army, is the result of an initiative signed by President Bush in January, 2002 which gives them a fast track to citizenship. This is coupled with the strong belief in the Mexican community of giving back to the country, and protecting the homeland, however misplaced that belief might be perceived by others in the case of Iraq.

Most people in Mexico and elsewhere in the Americas consider the term "American" descriptive of the hemisphere, not something exclusive to the United States. Christopher Columbus discovered America in Santo Domingo (Dominican Republic), after all, not in Washington, D.C. "I look forward to the day," Octavio Paz once

179

wrote, "when the United States will see itself as part of America, not all of it." *Todos somos americanos*, we are all Americans, including the oft-invaded, now-maligned Latin Americans whose sons and daughters fight our dirty wars abroad, while their parents receive not honor, but public abuse, at home. This might be a good time to remember our true past and all the people who share in it. Former president Bush remembers: his governorship and long-time residency in Texas (formerly an integral part of the Republic of Mexico) long ago convinced him. It is time for the conservative critics in his own party to open their history books and replace negative sound bites with thoughtful support for a intelligent and compassionate immigration bill, and for both sides to join in efforts to insure a truly "American" solution that is fair and just, that takes into consideration our complex history in this hemisphere, and is one that all our children can live with.

CHAPTER XIII: A DOGGY DOG WORLD – Re-thinking Educational Priorities

I've worked as a U.S. educator abroad for a good part of my life, for sixteen years as an Advanced Placement (AP) literature teacher in Mexico, and most recently as a consultant to the College Board in Latin America. This year I was invited by a group of educators in Bogotá, Colombia to reflect on the importance of the tasks we were assigning to our AP students. I welcomed the opportunity because it seemed to me a perfect forum for explaining what is right about education and how we can affirm it.

The substance of the AP literature exam is that the students are asked to carefully read selected passages from world literature, engage the works critically, and formulate essays which show careful analysis, comparative exegesis, and reflection. When I look around at other programs and other courses, the ambitions of parents for their children, and the goals of most students, I see that the intellectual rigor required in these courses is not demanded elsewhere in most school curricula, or in our daily lives as citizens. We have become mass consumers, and the purpose of education is seen by society as mere preparation for a lucrative job so that young people can continue the cycle of consumption, have an upscale car, a beautiful house, and healthy investments. This explains why it is projected that in the year 2010 there will be ten lawyers for every engineer. Why more than 60% of students are going into a "business" career, why fewer and fewer medical students choose to be general practitioners, and why humanities departments in universities are not flourishing.

Our society is anti-intellectual. Its heroes are entertainers, millionaires and athletes, not scholars. Consumption of "information" has replaced thoughtful reading; impulse for reflection; sound bites have taken the place of careful analysis; political correctness has replaced tolerance and understanding, and how one looks is more important that what one thinks. Most people simply have no time to think these days, and generally leave it to others, consuming ready-made opinions from the *Times* Op-Ed Page, or TV's "in-depth" reports on *Sixty Minutes* or *Anderson Cooper 360°*.

The rich possibilities of education have been relegated to the least common denominator of quasi-vocational (euphemistically called "professional") training with the result that our most promising graduates are being harnessed to the plow of multinational corporations and the ideology of the dollar without having had a chance to reflect on whether that is in fact their best choice as human beings. The educational system itself, driven as it is by corporate philosophies and strategies, by marketing principles, by bottom line test scores, by "exit criteria" for students and by "merit pay" for staff, is the largest contributor to the destruction of what education should be: an opportunity to encounter the complexities of the world in an organized fashion with a caring mentor, to develop a greater understanding of the principles underlying life, to reflect on one's values and on those of the society in which one lives, and to begin to make informed decisions as to what role one will play in that society, based on one's natural inclinations, skills and motivations.

False democratic ideals.

Schools are often encouraged by parents, by the pedagogical literature which pours out from academia (often written by people who don't teach or haven't taught in years), that elitism is a danger in the schools. They are told that education should be "democratic" and that there should be no honors courses, no division of students according to achievement or interests, and that advanced courses, if they are included in the curriculum at all, should be based on open admissions with no prerequisites. This has resulted, of course, in watered-down curricula in most public schools, supported by instructional packets and in-service projects designed to make the courses teacher-proof. It has resulted in curricula so dumbed-down that anybody with a credential, with little interest in reading, no depth in literature, mediocre skills as a writer, may and often does manage to "teach" literature courses, relying on "significant" excerpts from the textbook and the basic (yet often misleading) notes to teachers in the instructional guides.

The Advanced Placement Program is one of the few opportunities that exist for our students to think about issues, to reflect on values, culture and society, and to write thoughtful, analytical, comparative, descriptive or argumentative essays on what they read and understand. The Advanced Placement teacher, with a master's degree in his or her field, is a committed mentor who can lead the student to make informed decisions.

I have heard the program being called elitist and selective— even undemocratic—by some of my colleagues. While the first two adjectives may be applicable, as I will discuss later, there is nothing undemocratic about the selection process. In most international schools, the AP teacher announces the course offering for the coming year, and invites any student with the prerequisites to enroll, provided the student is motivated, disciplined, and committed to doing this level of study. Then the teacher offers a challenging summer assignment which, if the student completes it, is the ticket to entry into the class in the fall. The AP class is open to any student who is willing to work. But it is not for everybody. It is not for those without the interest, the motivation, or maturity to work independently. It is not for those who simply want the AP designation on their transcript without doing the work, or sitting for the qualifying exam. There is nothing undemocratic about that. Not everyone is equally motivated to play basketball, act, sing, debate, or run for class office. We don't have 50 class presidents, or a 100-member soccer team. Neither should AP classes be filled up with those who lack interest or motivation and indicate that they are unlikely to do the required work.

A clear and present danger.

After the tragic events of September 11, 2001, the United States was given an opportunity to reflect on its values, its foreign policy, its obligations to its citizens and its meaning as a civilized society. Instead, it allowed government leaders to turn a terrorist strike into an "act of war," thus legitimizing and giving nation-like status to a handful of criminals. It invaded Iraq based on intelligence manipulated to fit a preconceived agenda, and managed to kill tens of thousands of innocent civilians. It formulated a series of domestic security measures which violated at least five elements of the Bill of Rights guaranteed by our Constitution. It so intimidated journalists that the press became an instrument of propaganda. It made of Congress a willing presidential toady, and elevated its president's clichés to Churchillian status despite their empty content.

Many of our students, who were taught to be reflective, to use precise language, to be skeptical of bombast and Orwellian "doublespeak," were not caught so unaware. They saw, as did many teachers and thoughtful citizens of the U.S., and almost all educators overseas, that the government had been taken hostage by people who had made precise language their first victim.

They saw how the press has come to dichotomize public discourse in the U.S and how, despite its claims to be "free," the press itself is compromised by corporations that advertise in publications or pay for air time, by self-censorship, by partisan support of mainstream political candidates, and by uncritical acceptance of subjective reports from journalists "embedded" with the armed forces.

Domestic thinkers who disagreed with government policies during the Bush regime were considered liberal, leftist, Democrat at best—as pursuing an ideologically-based vendetta against the party in power, despite the fact that they might be centrist, unaligned or simply independent thinkers. Any criticism they might have had was thus divested of effect simply because it was from the opposition. A foreigner offering a criticism of U.S. policy was immediately characterized as anti-American, the criticism itself generally classified as "America bashing" and unworthy of rebuttal. Countries critical of U.S. policy were responded to by attacks on their "lack of gratitude" in the case of France, by their "unsavory history" in the case of Germany, or by a contemptuous reference to illegal immigration in the case of Mexico.

The lights are out.

I was in Costa Rica during that country's presidential elections in the final years of the Bush administration. As we were awaiting the election results on the TV in the hotel lounge, the network showed an interview with Secretary of Defense Donald Rumsfeld at the Washington Press Club.

Rumsfeld was asked what he thought about the New Leftist movements in Latin America, the ascendancy of Hugo Chávez in Venezuela and Evo Morales in Bolivia.

He said that all one had to do was look at satellite images from deep space of Korea at night. In South Korea one could see millions of lights reflecting a vibrant and free economy, whereas in North Korea it was mostly dark. "There," he said, "is the difference between a free economy and a command structure. As for Chávez," he continued, "one has to remember that Adolph Hitler was also freely elected, but he was certainly not a democratic leader."

The interviewer nodded sagely and went on to the next question. Several people watching the TV whooped in incredulity that Rumsfeld had said nothing about Latin America at all; each had their opinion about the Secretary's discourse, mostly based on ideology and mostly emotionally-charged. However, one young man commented: "*Non sequitur*, ignoring the question, *argumentum ad hominum*, false analogy. I'm afraid Mr. Rumsfeld never troubled himself to learn logic." And there it was. The kind of incisive observation that makes the difference between informed debate and knee-jerk response, between thoughtful citizens and ideological sheep.

The young man went on to say that the Secretary obviously had nothing to say about Latin America because there was not enough clear data available to his administration that did not run counter to his preconceived ideological positions. Thus, the Secretary ignored the question and changed the ground of the argument. He did this in two ways: he made a comparison of a totalitarian government (North Korea) with a democratic one (Venezuela), assuming the reader would associate the two because of socialist elements in their respective economies. However, as any schoolboy knows, many democratic socialist republics (whether Canada, Sweden, Chile or Denmark) are indeed democracies.

To run roughshod over this perception, he compared Chávez to Hitler (*argumentum ad hominum*) in the hope that the listener might conclude that Venezuela's free elections resulted in an abuse of power and totalitarianism. Yet to most Venezuelans, who not only had a genuine choice in the election but later employed several direct democratic components in changing the constitution and then restoring the president after an attempted military coup (the original coup was applauded by the U.S. and the *New York Times*), Venezuela is far more democratic than the military-industrial superpower to the north which is controlled by a plutocracy that every four years offers the public a circus in which two wealthy men, so totally compromised by the armaments industry and multinationals that they cannot or will not address major issues of concern to their constituents, vie for executive power.

A Doggy Dog World

In one of his last State of the Union addresses President Bush promised that his administration would provide training for 40,000 new Advanced Placement teachers in science and mathematics so that the U.S. would be more competitive in the world. As a former AP teacher I thought it sad, especially for this president whose facility with language and mastery of cohesive thought are conspicuous by their paucity, that he should not advocate training for at least twenty thousand AP English and humanities teachers as well.

For we teachers and university professors who read the AP exams each year, and decide that 48% of those who sit for the exam are not qualified by their reading skills, their logic, their ability to express a simple point of view and document their position, and thus go on to receive poor grades of 0, 1 or 2, the need seems obvious. One of the ways some of us amuse ourselves during breaks is recounting the malapropisms and logical imbroglios the students write. An interesting one which forms the metaphor for this essay came from a student who wished to express the fierce competition in global society. "It is," the student wrote, "a doggy dog world."

Noam Chomsky once wrote that "The structure of language not only determines thought, but reality itself." So what was that student's thought? What is the reality of that student's world? It was not the "dog eat dog" of the Social Darwinists to which the student was referring. That might have been a cogent thought and could even have been illustrated by references to Jack London's work or the philosophy of positivism. But "doggy dog world" leads to nothing but absurdity and futility. It is a world without meaning in which one thing is quite as good or bad as another, and there is not much one can do to change it.

It is said that Adolf Hitler once invited all of the great minds of the Third Reich to a meeting in Berlin. Present were the best chemists, the best physicists, the best architects. They were asked only one question. What is the best way to bring about the Final Solution, i.e., the elimination of the Jews?

The danger in designing an educational system where the best minds are funneled into the teaching of science and mathematics, while history, literature, philosophy and psychology are minimalized or discounted, is that of creating a soul-less society in which the truly significant questions are no longer asked. A society in which the manipulation of matter and quantifiable activities are the only ones rewarded, where everything is subject to the test of the marketplace, where human values are discounted, and where no one asks "why." It is a society in which politicians can speak nonsense and be quoted seriously in the press, where corporate slogans empty of content ("Coke is the real thing") can be accepted as truth, where even the formally educated are untrained in—or indifferent to—logical analysis of discourse, where planning a society is more a matter of architecture than of human relations, and where life is simply a chemical process that can be manipulated without moral reservations.

The Essence of Stupidity

Milan Kundera, author of *The Unbearable Lightness of Being*, once wrote that "stupidity does not give way to science, technology, modernity, progress; on the contrary it progresses right along with progress." By stupidity he did not mean ignorance, which is a lack of knowledge. Training and study can give us knowledge, but we can still be stupid. Kundera said that "Modern stupidity means not ignorance, but the **non-thought** of received ideas." The laziness, the shrug of the shoulders that allows us to accept ideas without testing them first, is what Kundera was addressing. All areas of human development partake of this kind of stupidity, but the irony is that the one area where it should be absent, education, is where it flourishes like a rank weed.

The first of these received ideas in education is that it is the job of teachers to serve their governmental, religious and civic hierarchies by espousing the ideological certitudes of those institutions. Can you imagine suggesting that to Socrates, to Aristotle, to Galileo, to John Henry Newman, to William James, to Einstein, to any teachers of the past whom we respect? All of them saw the job of the teacher as one of questioning ideological certitude, contradicting overly simplistic formulations, and encouraging their students to do so. Galileo did not spend his time praising the hierarchical Church and the wonders of an earth-centered universe. Socrates did not jump on the bandwagon to sing the praises of Athenian democracy. Einstein turned the world of physics downside up and outside in. And William James, the prominent

Harvard lecturer and philosopher, called teaching no science at all but an art, the art of confrontation.

The purpose of government schools or public schools in any country is the propagandizing of future citizens. Students are not taught real history (although it is called that); they are taught a corrupted nationalistic version. The purpose of teaching history in government-supported schools is to present a version of that country's development which will inspire unquestioning loyalty and civic obedience. The history of your country, the students are told, is the history of a sometimes imperfect, but always evolutionary advance of the human spirit.

It is only when we read another country's version of similar events that we have some perspective, and see that much of what we've been taught is errant nonsense. However, since most public high schools do not teach the histories of other countries, such comparisons and understandings are usually not forthcoming. It is only in AP courses such as comparative politics, the study of foreign languages and cultures, world history and cultural geography that good teachers have an opportunity to present them. AP students are exposed to studies of comparative governments and cultures, to alternative and contradictory histories. They are encouraged to ferret out the truth when possible, and to accept ambiguity when it is not.

English versus Language Arts

The second perceived truth is that simple language is for simple people and that in these sophisticated times, if teachers want to be respected, they need to use more elegant language to describe what they do. It used to be that we taught reading and writing in grammar school and middle school, and then literature and composition in high school. Now in most schools children are taught "language arts" for all twelve years. "Language arts," now there's an epithet to turn the stomach of a future Octavio Paz, a future Joyce Carol Oates. And just what is meant by the term? The art of translation, the art of editing, the art of comprehending comparative literature? The art of producing short stories and essays in creative writing workshops? Not really. It is actually reading and writing with a high-sounding name, with the tacit and fatuous assumption of textbook editors that writing literature is something we can all do. Read a descriptive excerpt from a short story and then write your own version. Read an accessible and didactic verse and then write your own version. The teacher will correct the spelling and grammar in the first, and help you with the meter in the second. Reading complete stories, novels, essays and collections of poetry is antithetical to the language arts practicum. Check out the textbooks and you'll see. Language arts texts prefer quick visuals, an excerpt from the author, a one-page response, or five-paragraph essay from the student. If a student learns anything about literature, about the culture, history, philosophy or conflicts of values which inform a text, it is because the teacher has gone well beyond the language arts textbook. But most don't. Which is why the system that produced this neologism has less than 80% who formally study a language other than English, 60% who have never read a 19th century British novel, 80% who have never read the original historical documents upon which their own government is based. Nor, in my observation, has this system produced many decent high school writers because at their age they see an unbridgeable gap between what has been done and what they would do. They have not developed understanding or love for literature because they have read only polished excerpts which they cannot possibly duplicate. They do not see the scaffolding behind the passage which their less-skilled minds could attempt if only they were taught the work in its entirety.

Let's go back to reading and writing, grammar and spelling. Let's go back to literature and composition. The words we use to describe what we do should reflect what we actually do. Let's go back to saying what we mean and meaning what we say.

The Right to Fail

The third bit of received wisdom which is generally unchallenged says that all students have an inalienable right to the best education and the teacher's job is to serve them. Wrong again. In an equitable society students and parents should have the right to access the best education. That means a seat should be saved for the student. But once he or she is in that seat, education becomes a mutual endeavor. I am reminded of the story of the Chinese master with a wonderful reputation who has just been assigned to a new village school. One of the boys decides to test him, to see if he is truly as wise and brilliant as has been reported. He says to his friend, "I will take a sparrow and hold it behind my back. I will ask him whether the sparrow is alive or dead. If he says, 'Dead,' I will produce it and say, 'No, master; you are wrong. It is alive.' If the master says that the bird is alive, I will twist its neck and kill it, then produce its corpse saying, 'No, master; it is dead.' Then the whole village will see that this teacher is not as wise as we have been told."

Well, the teacher arrives. And the boy approaches him with a group of his cronies and a dozen villagers eager to see the master tested. The boy says to the teacher, "Master, I have a bird in my hands behind my back. Is the bird alive or is it dead?" The master looks the boy in the eye and then he says, "I do not know, my son, because the bird is in **your** hands."

There are two important things this story makes clear. First, the student has a responsibility for his or her education and, second, the teacher is the master not the servant. Failure to do homework, failure to respectfully interact with peers and with teachers, failure to complete readings or turn in work on time, means that the student has chosen to forfeit his or her opportunity for that period. In the Educational Bill of Rights we need to add: students have the right to fail; the birds are in their hands.

A colleague reading over these words remarked that I was something of an elitist in education. Elitist is an interesting word. It did not exist in most dictionaries until the Cold War period and then it was a word coined by totalitarian governments to refer to intellectuals who were dangerous to the State. It is interesting that we never use the words with athletes. We don't call Michael Jordan or Mike Tyson elitists. We don't use it with musicians or movie stars. No one would call Shakira an elitist or Robert De Niro an elitist. It is an anti-intellectual term based on insecurity. It is part of the pseudo-democratic mentality which infuses many schools. This is the credo that says all students should be treated the same with no exceptions, regardless of their work ethic, their attitude or their talents. They tell us that it is best to do away with pre-AP, Advanced Placement, and Honors courses, as well as the National Honor Society which recognizes academic excellence, leadership and intellectual integrity. We are told that these types of selections divide the kids, replace cooperation with competitiveness, and isolate the nerds in the school instead of integrating them.

But the same people who suggest this would never do away with the athletic teams, with football, basketball, skateboarding competitions, school plays and talent shows in which even smaller percentages of children are singled out for recognition. It is only in the area of academics that this epithet "elitist" is applied. And how ironic, how shameful for us, that it is used in education where academic excellence should be the hallmark of our profession.

Latin America and AP Programs

In Latin America we have seen a significant growth of Advanced Placement courses in the past decade. The results are apparent to me as I travel throughout the region, and were plainly illustrated by the young man in Costa Rica who used logic as a scalpel to expose the fallacies in Secretary Rumsfeld's speech. The results are also apparent at universities in Colombia, in Uruguay, Paraguay, Argentina, Dominican Republic, Costa Rica and Mexico where students are able to sort through ideological extremes and approach controversial issues with open minds. No longer are groups conservative or liberal, Marxist or corporatist. More and more students are eclecticists in philosophy and pragmatists in economics, looking at the best combination of elements to serve the interests of their country or region. It is refreshing.

I know such students are at campuses in the United States as well, but the nasty partisanship of media "stars" such as Lou Dobbs and Bill O'Reilly, which has infested every level of political discourse (as recently evidenced by the debate over immigration), leaves intelligent students with few options beyond saying, "It is more complex, more interesting than that." There is little to support them against what Cardinal Newman called "the blundering discourtesy of less educated minds, who like blunt weapons, tear and hack instead of cutting clean, who mistake the point in argument, misconceive their adversary, and leave the question more involved than they find it." Fewer and fewer college students are taking philosophy classes. And economics courses in the U.S. are already so ideologically tainted that studying macro-economics there in the hope of understanding diverse economies is akin to studying St. Augustine and St. Paul in a Jesuit theology course with the hopes of getting an insight into comparative religions.

What is so refreshing to me about Latin American universities today is their openness, and their emphasis on humanities-based education. Quietly in some cases, more dramatically in others, new experiments in mixed economies are being tried; efforts are being made to create more inclusive societies; questions concerning class and equitable distribution of wealth are openly discussed; the public benefits of privatizing national resources are being seriously questioned, and education—though still far from being universal—is seen more and more as a tool of individual and social development, not as a means of creating ideological uniformity and unthinking consumerism. They have a long way to go, quite obviously, but at least they are going in the right direction. And in a "doggy dog world," that is quite significant.

CHAPTER XIV: THE SUNSET OF U.S. EMPIRE BUILDING - The Rise of a New Latin America

A century and a half of interventions, costly miscalculations, even outright invasions, did not do much to push Latin America away from its sometimes passive-aggressive, sometimes envious, but always dependent relationship with the United States. It took the generalized failure of neoliberalism, coupled with four years of U.S. indifference to the region following the events of 9/11 and the unilateral megalomania of pre-emptive war, for Latin Americans to decide it was time to determine their own destiny.

Increased poverty, the failure of the Washington Consensus and the IMF, privatization and corporate greed, the marginalization of large groups of people—in what Washington touted as democratic reform and free trade—led to a gradual rejection of advice from U.S. economic and political experts pushing the neoliberal agenda throughout the hemisphere. The perceived hypocrisy of the United States government which, while condemning torture by the Latin American military in the past, exceeded the worst examples of it at Abu Ghraib; the failure to consult allies on a massive preemptive invasion; the callousness of a government which deported Central Americans during one of the worst hurricanes in history and then failed to provide significant humanitarian aid, all contributed to the loss of U.S. moral authority in the region.

It used to be that the more the U.S. blundered, the angrier Latin Americans would become. Now, they are mostly grateful. Global television satellites carry pictures and narratives describing a government they no longer envy, and behaviors they find deplorable. The governmental indifference they saw as they viewed the poor in New Orleans slighted by elected officials, the incompetence which was apparent as they viewed $300 million in mobile homes abandoned at an Arkansas airport, the intransigence which they observe as they watch U.S. marines dying in what is essentially a civil conflict in an Arab country, the violation of basic human rights of which they read as U.S. citizens have their phones tapped to provide more "national security," have all made Latin Americans turn inward in recent years and rely on themselves, and on their neighbors with whom they share common cultural backgrounds and common goals. It has also helped them to avoid the ideological dichotomies and rhetorical traps which are so ubiquitous in U.S. public discourse, and to openly question the sacredness of strong executive democracy, global security, free trade, privatization, and creation of more ownership wealth; while taking a second look at socialism, community action, regional alliances, Bolivarian revolution, public resources, common space, state utilities, and equitable distribution of wealth. They have moved beyond traditional formulations and clichés, and toward a more pragmatic approach to true democracy "of the people, by the people, and for the people," in the proto-socialist language of Abraham Lincoln.

The result has been more autonomous action in recent years: characterized by more self-reliance by Latin American republics, the growth of regional alliances, the use of true democratic instruments such as referendum and recall to change a constitution, unseat presidents who were toadies of the IMF, and to curtail the abuses of state power. It has made political leaders more responsive to the people, resulting in a new recognition of indigenous rights, discarding IMF guidelines and World Bank suggestions, discounting debts which were bleeding the populace of social services and basic subsidies, and refusing to privatize water and other resources which properly belong to the citizens themselves, and are their legacy to their children. It can be seen in the almost unanimous condemnation of the war with Iraq by Latin Americans, a general distrust of the hemispheric security alliance proposed by Washington, and a rejection of corporate theories maximizing profit at the expense of people—seen most significantly with Wal-Mart, which has devastated the U.S. landscape and undermined small businesses, but has been rejected by much of Latin America and may be forced to close its doors permanently in some regions because of declining profits.

A Simple Corrective

What the U.S. government and pundits (both conservative and liberal) characterize as a Leftist movement and a resurgence of Marxism in the region, most Latin Americans view as a simple corrective, much like that implemented during the era of Franklin Roosevelt after the disaster of the Great Depression and the incompetence of the Hoover Administration. What North Americans view as unholy alliances such as those being formed between Venezuela and Cuba, most Latin Americans see as practical solutions to real problems of survival, no less pressing than those of the United States when it formed a 1940s alliance with Russia to ensure the survival of its people. What North Americans see as disorderly and chaotic, for example the teacher strikes in Mexico, the indigenous blockades of highways in Guatemala, the removal of presidents in Argentina, the constitutional reforms in Venezuela; most Latin Americans see as true democratic processes where the people are finally having a real voice in governance, and correcting plutocratic republics which have long been tilted in favor of inherited wealth and privilege—much as our U.S. activist labor organizations operated as a corrective against the abuses of the Carnegies and Vanderbilts in the early part of the 20th century. For too long Latin Americans have been denied their own history while the U.S. forced them to operate as addenda to the North American story. Now all that has changed. Latin

Americans are writing this new chapter of continental history and they do not want U.S. editors or spellcheckers involved in the process.

Erosion of Neoliberalism

Grassroots reactions against globalization policies, promoted by U.S. multinationals and the IMF, have been having their effect throughout Latin America. The voices of organized labor, the unrepresented working poor, university students, indigenous people, environmentalists, professors, middle and leftist political candidates, are finally being heard. The regional press, which used to call any such opposition "globophobia" and demean the protestors as unorganized and without a clear agenda, has now begun to report more seriously, occasionally even editorializing on their behalf. Moreover, the protests are having concrete results as more and more governments are beginning to see the futility of trying to lead without "the consent of the governed."

A Broader Democracy

When Abraham Lincoln gave his celebrated Gettysburg Address, the oft-quoted "four score and seven" referred to the American Revolution, and the ideal of equality defined in the Declaration of its principles. He observed that the Republic had failed. That was why they were meeting on this "great battlefield" in

Pennsylvania to dedicate a massive graveyard with tens of thousands of dead on both sides.

The failure of the hemisphere's first revolution and the claim of its Declaration that "all men are created equal" was apparent by the 1860s with 13% of the population enslaved (47% in the South). Lincoln wondered whether "this nation or any other nation so conceived and so dedicated" could endure. Even then, of course, indigenous people were not even in the equation, nor were women. While the Republic was a government "of the people," that is, ostensibly a democratic republic, it was certainly not **for** the people, except for white men, nor **by** the people, except by the landed gentry, merchants, the plutocrats of Washington and their minions. He hoped on that battlefield in 1863 that the country would experience "a new birth of freedom."

What we are seeing in Latin America is exactly that: a new birth of freedom, a more inclusive democracy. We are also seeing the end of ideology, and a different kind of social enterprise. The new models are certainly not socialism as it was known in the past, with indigenous workers excluded from the process, with bureaucracies and party bosses calling the shots. They seem instead to be genuine attempts at government by the people and for the people, demanding that political leaders, business owners and corporations behave responsibly and in the best interests of the governed; not condoning privatization of a country's natural resources, interested in neighbor alliances, encouraging indigenous participation at every level and condemning the cronyism common to U.S. politics where lucrative contracts are awarded to friends and pristine lands are exploited at the behest of Washington lobbyists on the payrolls of coal, gas and oil companies.

The Sanctity of Private Property

The U.S. has expressed concerns about investments in the region and has invoked the sanctity of private property which appears to have been violated with workers taking over an abandoned hotel, a private school and a factory in Argentina and running them successfully. It has also raised this issue when indigenous people reclaimed untenanted hectares in Brazil and Bolivia, or forced corporate timber cutters to leave ancestral lands. However, in the case of Argentina, these properties were deserted by absentee landlords; in the case of Brazil and Bolivia, these ancestral lands were either left fallow or at imminent risk of being denuded and destroyed.

Meanwhile, in the United States, good houses and profitable small businesses are condemned so that Wal-Marts can be built, in clear abuse of the true spirit of eminent domain statutes. In addition, this same company and others like it, having destroyed businesses and put people out of their homes, often abandon their own sites within a few years to avoid paying municipal taxes.

Who is instructing whom on the sanctity of private property? Ownership of property is a right which carries obligations. When property is neglected and becomes an eyesore and a health hazard, it is the right of the people in that neighborhood to take action. When a public forest is being denuded, streams polluted, and fertile lands expropriated by international corporations to grow soybeans for China, it is certainly the right of indigenous people to protect their heritage. This is democracy and this is what we are seeing in Latin America. In the U.S., Wal-Mart's use of its economic clout to manipulate the courts into condemning perfectly good homes and businesses is a clear corruption of the system, and clearly undemocratic. The U.S. invocation of the sacredness of property shibboleth is clear hypocrisy.

Peace Movement

The demilitarization movement in Costa Rica, spearheaded by Nobel Laureate Oscar Arias, is an example of the winds of change in Latin America. I spoke with Arias in San José two years ago and he said that he envisioned Costa Rica as a regional leader in demilitarization, which would set an international example of peace, regional cooperation, social welfare, and environmental efforts. Costa Rica has replaced its armed forces with a national brigade (focused mostly on rescue operations, border and airport security, and disaster relief), and has thus reserved millions of dollars for its education budget, and spearheaded international aid efforts and peace initiatives (Arias brokered the treaty in Central America which ended a decade and a half of war, and has more recently been involved with the Honduras accords after the military removed a sitting president).

Meanwhile, Costa Rica leads the world in environmental custodianship, while the U.S. Congress debates such measures as whether or not it should ravage its pristine arctic habitats for the last remaining drops of oil.

Mexico's refusal to support the U.S. invasion of Iraq, and most of Latin America's reluctance to be part of the Security Alliance of the Americas, its distrust of U.S. military intervention including a century and a half of invasions throughout the Americas, leaves only seven countries out of the thirty-four in Latin America as reluctant supporters of the U.S. presence in Iraq, and that support is largely based on trade accords not ratified by the populace.

Most people in Latin America felt that the Administration's use of 9/11 as the *casus belli* for invasion of Iraq made as much sense as invading Canada in retaliation for the Oklahoma City bombing. They saw the 9/11 attack, like that by the home-grown terrorists in Oklahoma, as one perpetrated by individuals and not by a sovereign State, to which the logical response should have been to investigate and track down the perpetrators and their supporters who, the world knows, happened to be Saudis not Iraquis.

The latest Washington-inspired proposal for the Latin American region, an "Inter-American Convention Against Terrorism" seems to most people in the southern hemisphere as patently absurd. Central America has real and present problems with public safety in the form of trained-in-the-U.S. Latino gangs which have infested their communities and are a far more real and much more imminent danger than Osama Bin Laden. The U.S. seems to have little to offer in terms of help for the problem of these hemispheric terrorists. People in Venezuela and Brazil are much more concerned with problems of crime and delinquency fostered by inherited social problems, than they are with U.S. threats from the Middle East. To them, the hemispheric security alliance is just another U.S. nationalistic plan which will draw off funds, security personnel and technology from areas where they would be most effective for their own citizenry.

Current U.S. Latin American Policy

There is no consistent U.S. policy for Latin America. The most significant aspect of our policy has been pervasive neglect in recent years. There has been, of course, promotion of trade agreements beneficial to international corporations and U.S. economic interests, the creation of *maquiladoras* (which, while destroying the environment and putting female workers at risk, ensure low costs to U.S. consumers), and a refusal to end U.S. agricultural subsidies, thus depriving Latin American farmers of a fair price for their produce. In some cases such as Venezuela and Nicaragua, there has been leverage applied to the electoral process, in Paraguay an installation of U.S. troops, in Colombia a massive amount of funding to impede drug traffic which has also hindered the growth of leftist opposition, while at the same time ensuring the relative immunity of right wing vigilantes. For the rest, mostly ignorance and neglect to such an extent that few Latin Americans take the U.S. seriously, just as no one takes an elephant seriously. One has respect, of course, for its size and power as an entity, but not as an intellectual, cultural or moral force, and certainly not for its leadership abilities.

President Obama's recent participation in the Conference on the Americas in Port of Spain was heralded as a step in repairing these relationships. However, its effectiveness was diluted considerably by the U.S. media's concern over his receiving a gift book from President Chávez, and his ostensible overtures to Cuba (which was not even invited to participate in the conference). Despite what U.S. pundits have said about the administration's new concern for a Latin American partnership, President Obama's response to the gift he received from Chávez was noteworthy. The book, *The Open Veins of Latin America* by Eduardo Galeano, is one of the best historical analyses of the region. It has sold millions of copies and is required reading in most international studies programs. When asked about it, President Obama's replied, "Just because I accepted the gift, doesn't mean I intend to read it." Whether his response was dictated by a need to mollify his critics on the right or by simple ignorance of the book's content, it was unfortunate.

The Colombian Exception

Despite some justifiable criticism of Plan Colombia since its inception, the continued presence of right-wing security squads and human rights abuses in rural areas, Colombia has gone from a war-ravaged, drug-infested, insecure country in the 90s to one of the most prosperous and generally safe regions in Latin America. I have visited every major city there and the capitol a half dozen times over the past eighteen years. I was impressed by the cosmopolitan excitement of Bogotá, which compares favorably with Boston in term of cultural activities, music, museums, documentary film-making, fine universities, and continental cuisine. The young people are stylish, educated, and multilingual. It has a strong middle class and, while it has its poor, there is little evidence of the homelessness and beggars which one can see any day in Washington or San Francisco.

Medellín, once considered the "murder capital" of the world, is now one of the most attractive cities in the Americas. It has the feel of an Austrian metropolis surrounded by pristine farms, lushly wooded hills, and crisp mountain air. It has a well-maintained infrastructure, with clean streets, excellent public transportation, and one of the most prestigious medical universities in the Americas. Medellín is, in fact, so safe that it was where former Secretary of State Rice chose to visit on her last official trip to the region.

Much of Colombia's success is due to its president, Alvaro Uribe, whose family was victimized by drug-related violence; he has since been committed to its eradication. But, in fairness, it is more than that. There also has been a genuine effort by the U.S. Department of State to work in a cooperative way with local officials in the country, not only to help contain the violence and eradicate drug cultivation, but also to eliminate corruption in the police and armed forces, and to secure the already-strong educational system. While engaged in these activities, U.S. representatives in the region have also exhibited respect for the culture, and there have been virtually no negative incidents involving U.S. personnel.

Colombian universities **are** now attracting new students from all over the world; secondary schools are involved in the Advanced Placement program; the president has implemented a plan to stop the brain-drain of the best and brightest and is also offering financial incentives for the 4,000 or so Colombians with doctorate degrees now living abroad to return to their native country.

In 2007 a local newspaper conducted a survey asking whether readers felt more secure now than a decade ago, whether they trusted the police, and whether the president was doing a good job. Affirmative responses were in the 70th percentile. That same year I went down to visit a school in Barranquilla and I was again impressed by the quality of education, the determination of young people to get ahead, and the enthusiasm of those who attend the (sometimes free) concerts offered by Juanes and Shakira, two Colombians whose international acclaim and wealth have not distracted them from their obligations to their homeland, and who have made significant financial and moral commitments to building peace and aiding Colombian youth. Shakira's *Pies Descalzos* (Barefeet) Foundation has given aid to thousands of children displaced by civil wars and violence; Juanes has brought global attention to landmine removal, and has turned paramilitary rifles into guitars to highlight the disarmament process.

I have read (and have myself written) a great deal of criticism of the U.S. in Latin America, most of it justified. However, for those who criticize our cooperative efforts of the past decade with Colombians to work for a safer and more prosperous country, I would say come to Medellín, come to Bogotá. You will see what can be accomplished.

The Bolivarian Alternative

Just as Abraham Lincoln invoked the hope of a "new birth of freedom" in the United States, José Martí, hero of Cuban independence, also called for a "second independence" in the Americas, this one from U.S. dominance. Now, President Hugo Chávez seems poised to make that happen. The new "alliance for progress," popularly known as ALBA (Bolivarian Alternative for the Americas), is a plan for regional alliances and sharing of resources. It has resulted in a Development Bank of the South and a Latin American Development Fund to replace dependence on foreign capital and expand Latin American trade with Europe and Asia. For Venezuela, it has also spearheaded the construction of 600 comprehensive health clinics with Cuban assistance, and sent 30,000 Cuban medical technicians to train cadres of health workers. In Cuba, aspiring Venezuelan doctors and nurses will receive free training at Cuba's prestigious School of Medical Sciences where 43,000 students from 17 countries (including 71 from the U.S.) are now working to get their medical degrees. In exchange, the Venezuelan government will provide 90,000 gallons of oil a day to energy-deprived Cuba, and invest in Cuban electricity production and oil refining.

Meanwhile, energy sector agreements between Venezuela, Argentina, Bolivia, Brazil, Chile and Uruguay have been enacted which include PetroCaribe for the entire Caribbean region. In addition, Mercosur, the South American trade block consisting of Argentina Brazil, Paraguay and Uruguay (Bolivia, Chile and Peru are associate members), is poised to induct Venezuela as a member. It is also considering Cuba as an associate member. With all this in mind, it is worth pointing out that, despite U.S. efforts to discredit Cuba in the region and in the international arena, Cuba now has diplomatic relations with 32 of the 34 Latin American nations, the only exceptions being El Salvador and Costa Rica.

The Rise of A New Latin America

Latin America is poised to become more independent, making regional alliances, promoting a more participatory democracy, with more rights for indigenous peoples, and more use of referendum and recall by the people to push through social legislation or remove corrupt leaders. Socialism will be regional in nature and look quite different from its historical forms (even Cuba's in the past): a bit more like Franklin Roosevelt's New Deal in some aspects, a bit like direct democracy in others. Labor unions will merge into companies where labor and management share decision making, or even form worker-owned companies. There will be more worker rights in terms of on-site health care, on-site day care, and worker-managed retirement investments. Vacant land and abandoned buildings (from failed Wal-Marts to warehouses abandoned by absentee landlords) will continue to be expropriated and made productive.

Government leaders will demand more corporate responsibility from users of the environment or put their legitimacy and tenancy in office at risk. Natural gas, petroleum, water and other national treasures will remain the property of the people and be managed by the State or as cooperatives.

The United States will become less and less influential in the region as countries form local partnerships, and trade blocs for negotiations with China, the European Union and Southeast Asia. Investment in education will increase with some of the smaller states developing (much as Ireland has over the past twenty years) into significant economic entities, raising the quality of life for their citizens. As Costa Rica has already done, some will abandon armies and armaments and invest those funds in education and social development. Those states with no natural enemies will also become more important on the international scene by offering advice to other nations wishing to dismantle military institutions whose primary function has been to control a marginalized populace.

Countries which have weapons of mass destruction (U.S., China, North Korea, Great Britain, France, India, and Pakistan) will find the burdens of "defense" expensive, redundant and superfluous as the years go on. The real threat to the social order and the average person's security on the planet will come from those nations with the most marginalized people and, while most of those threats will be internal (gang violence, crime), some will be external (international terrorism). Nevertheless, experience from the Latin American examples will be convincing: these problems will be far better handled by trained police forces and international security arrangements than by occupying armies, missile strikes and bombing of civilians.

Latin America will continue to be a world leader in literature, music, filmmaking, architecture, sculpture and painting. The region will produce new works of political and social thought, explore new dimensions in philosophy and rewrite the history of the hemisphere. It will become one of the most important locations for studies in medicine, pure and applied science, engineering, and—most importantly—the humanities. While the U.S. may invest, in "more advanced science and math" initiatives," Latin America will balance the teaching of the sciences with investments in the humanities. Time and time again local leaders and the independent press in Latin America have cited the need for citizens to think critically, to analyze their societies, to develop an appreciation of their rich cultures, and to help create a better world. They know that a society composed only of scientists, mathematicians and engineers will not give them that. A truly educated populace is one that can take its leaders to task when they offer absurdities, can form arguments to disrobe injustice, and can instill respect in its children for many different cultures. Such a society would be multicultural and multilingual, it would value humanity over property, and culture over development. In the words of Mexican poet Jaime Sabines, *Otros saben las palabras del canto, nosotros cantamos.* "Others know the words of the song, but we sing." Throughout Latin America, those songs are being heard.

Guadalajara, Mexico. 2009

ABOUT THE AUTHOR

Michael Hogan is the author of sixteen books, including a collection of short stories, six books of poetry, collected essays on teaching in Latin America, a novel, and a history of the Irish battalion in Mexico which formed the basis for an MGM movie starring Tom Berenger. His work has appeared in many journals such as the *Paris Review*, the *Harvard Review*, *Z-Magazine*, *Political Affairs* and the *Monthly Review*. He is currently director of the AP University Recognition Initiative for the College Board in Latin America.

Dr. Hogan has given workshops and presentations at over sixty conferences in the United States, Mexico, Canada, Central and South America and the Caribbean. In addition to his work in Latin America for the past sixteen years, Dr. Hogan is a former consultant on institutional programs for the National Endowment for the Arts, a consultant for the Irish Embassy in Mexico, and for the land mine removal initiative in Nicaragua. He also works with Homies Unidos on gang prevention and rehabilitation, and has served the U.S. federal courts as an expert witness on asylum cases from Central America.

His many awards include the gold medal of the Mexican Sociedad de Geografía y Estadísticas, a citation for meritorious service from the Office of Overseas Schools, U.S. Department of State, the

Grace Stoddard Literary Fellowship, the Ben Franklin Award 2000, and an NEA Creative Writing Fellowship.

Home page: www.drmichaelhogan.com

LaVergne, TN USA
28 October 2009
162234LV00002B/26/P